THE OTHER PAULINE

A Story of Courage and Determination For Identity

#1 Best Selling Co-Author
of *Mom Magic* and *Becoming An Unstoppable Woman Entrepreneur*

ISBN: 978-1-960136-32-9

Dedication

To all of you who believed in me when I didn't and to my mother-in-law, the other Pauline. XO

Foreword

I came into this world scared, unaware, vulnerable, and alone. I chose my mom and dad because their family's needed me more than they realized. These two families, Tellier (mom) and Aguesse (dad), encouraged and believed in me to start healing the ancestral lines that traumatized generation after generation of their lineage. They were unaware of how healing would happen, so they put their Catholic faith in me to navigate the waters of life and find the answers. With the knowledge I acquired through tantric healing, I've learned that scientific evidence explains how the feelings of abandonment and loneliness were predisposed in my DNA. There have been many challenges that derailed me at times, but I always got back up and persevered. This is why I was chosen. A combination of courage, self-determination, and faith provided a safe cocoon so I could blossom when I was ready. I had to live my life and learn through my experiences in order to help future generations understand how we can rewrite the history of two families together. I write my story for you now, with the knowledge of who I am after fifty years of the unknown, untruths, overcoming challenges of abuse, rape, divorce, suicidal ideologies, and abandonment. Why? So that my voice can be heard and by telling my story, I attempt to help others not feel alone, like I was. To explain how even when it feels like you are backed into a corner and you feel like there is no choice, there is always a choice, no matter how inconsequential it may look. Take my hand and come with me on my journey of growth, knowledge, and the instinct to know I always deserved better than what was presented to me. I learned through self-integrity to discover my true inner power. I encourage you to learn from my mistakes so that yours are not so great. I present to you *The Other Pauline*, with deep love and respect always.

Table of Contents

Foreword 3

Introduction 7

Chapter 1: Trauma Unravelled 10

Chapter 2: Empathizing with My World 15

Chapter 3: Learning How to Navigate the Waters of Life 21

Chapter 4: Forgivable Life Lessons.................................29

Chapter 5: The Many Parts of Me (Undiagnosed ADHD) 40

Chapter 6: Authentically Me....................................... 46

Chapter 7: The Truth Breaks Free 59

Chapter 8: After a Life of Being Cautious,
I Threw Caution to the Wind.......................................72

Chapter 9: "I Do… ???" 84

Chapter 10: What is Meant to Be, is Meant to Be 99

Chapter 11: Becoming an Alchemist.............................. 108

Chapter 12: Healing and Growing Beyond Imagination!............. 124

Introduction

Guided Journey Coaching & Consulting was created and inspired by Pauline Grouette, Dental Assistant turned entrepreneur. Over the past fifteen years Pauline noticed the need for more support in her field. She served from her heart on the dental assisting Board for six years, five of those being involved at an executive level. She found her voice on the board through educational committees, volunteering with the Manitoba Dental Association (sometimes as the *Tooth Fairy*), and being a crucial aid to change by-laws in support of the Manitoba Dental Field.

COVID-19 gave Pauline the opportunity to re-evaluate her life's purpose and establish her business. She knew intuitively that she was born for more by supporting men and women globally. Through a TV show called *Secrets, Lies and DNA Ties*, she began revealing never before discussed truths that had surfaced regarding the father she never knew. Awareness and clarity guided her to achieve surface level healing. She still did not feel whole. She was determined to get answers. More of her journey can be found as a guest on podcast platforms such as Spotify, Apple Podcasts, Google Podcasts, and more where she speaks authentically about her challenges and how she overcame them.

In 2021 that raw ache was still pushing at her from inside. She discusses how working with a tantric shaman brought her to healing on different levels and the enlightenment that came with it. Sharing parts of her life through radio interviews, magazine features, and as a co-author all helped to use her voice in ways she never dreamed possible. Becoming a Vision Board Facilitator for her clients' journeys enabled her to provide them direction, clarity, empowerment, and confidence to achieve new heights, just as she had. She became the top Certified Awareness Coach for 2023, by providing a safe space for people to understand that the opportunities were always available.

This book reflects the author's present recollections of experiences over time, and some details were omitted to protect those involved. Names were changed and events compressed for privacy of loved ones. By resurfacing and processing the emotions through tantric healing, writing this book has allowed Pauline closure and the ability to move forward to help her audience.

Life is a never ending journey of choice.

Who are you really?

Pauline's authenticity shows people that she has been in similar situations. Areas of abuse, rape, abandonment, single parenting, and loss of identity, amongst others. The repressed feelings that many adults were taught to avoid such as fear, anger, jealousy, resentment, and overwhelm came with societal judgement. Without realizing it people no longer know who they truly are.

Pauline will take you on a guided journey through her past, present, and future as she endeavours to create her finest self by discovering and reconnecting on a whole different level with herself and her ancestors. Her story will surface emotions as you find yourself relating to her. The young child who was required to explore and navigate through the world that she was chosen to reconstruct, while her ancestors and living family limited her growth due to their own fears. She is ending these fears now with her story.

Guided Journey Coaching offers:
- 1:1 coaching
- Group coaching
- Vision Board workshops
- Dental consulting
- Speaking engagements

- Masterclass "motivation through collaboration"
- Online courses

As Pauline continues to grow, so will you! Globally, being part of the ripple effect has already begun.

You always have a choice!

Sending love and gratitude,
Pauline Grouette
www.guidedjourneycoaching.ca

CHAPTER 1

Trauma Unravelled

My purpose on this Earth is to arrest the ancestral and generational trauma that has chained my family for centuries. My intention with this book is to empower everyone via different ways to heal, explain why we unintentionally (sometimes intentionally) put ourselves in difficult situations, and provide comfort knowing that you are not alone and always have a choice in every situation. Each challenge provided crucial and pivotal actions for me emotionally, physically, and spiritually, which you will learn as I bring you with me on my journey of healing and self-discovery. I will admit that I grew up when the thought of speaking to a therapist or psychiatrist was still taboo, and coaching was not even associated with mental health yet. I was able to find this new path with the help of my ancestral inner compass and tantric practices. I learned that my inner compass is very powerful. I didn't always feel this way. The confidence and self-belief that I was born with was slowly taken away. An innocent comment about the way I looked and behaved and not being allowed to show or express hard emotions like anger and sadness caused them to be more and more repressed. A large part of my journey was allowing these emotions to surface so that I could process them properly and give them the respect required so that I was able to move on and help others do the same. I learned that subconsciously (and in my DNA), traumas from previous generations haunted me and broke me down. I forgot on a conscious level how strong I really was, until I was reminded.

Having tried many different healing modalities, tantric was the one that called to me and guided me in a more progressive way. I knew nothing about tantric healing except that it involved sexual masculine and feminine energies, which made me very nervous. I had reached a point in my life where I decided to go all in and trust in the divine energies of the Mother Universe. Tantric is a spiritual East Indian tradition that focuses on the manifestation of the divine energy of oneness. It is not widely known in the Western world, and there are a lot of misconceptions. Tantric practices have changed not only my life but those of generations to come. Meditative study and tantric practices taught me to provide peace to my ancestors so they could rest. Limiting beliefs and trauma happened way before I was born. Ideas of not being good enough, leading to perfectionism, and expecting the same from everyone around me, made me slowly become exactly who I didn't want to become—someone who was never fully satisfied with almost everything around me. Luckily, I was able to turn this around, and this determination to always do better softened where necessary. I was unaware of how deep these inner traumas were. I understand that I can never truly get away from trauma, though I learned how to navigate the waters to make better decisions, which in turn brought better results; like a domino effect.

Being a history buff, I knew about societal pressures from many different centuries and decades, though I thought those were in the past and did not affect me today. Boy, was I wrong! I did not understand how all the challenges that my ancestors went through, like wars, depression, and feminist challenges which limited females in my family, were carried forward inside of me. As humans, we inherit so much more than simply the genetic DNA traits from our ancestors. As discovered in epigenetics, we also carry the DNA traumas from centuries before. Epigenetics is the study of how your behavior and environments can change gene expression rather than alteration of the genetic code itself. Our ancestral lineage carries emotional and psychological baggage that we do not see, similar to termed as emotional abuse today. Generational trauma and curses were not widely spoken of, at least not in my family. It is very difficult to comprehend the layers we have been born with. To paraphrase the words of my tantric shaman, Amba Kahly Su: like a computer, the hardware our body comes with is our DNA. This is the programming within us and how we present ourselves to the world on a surface level. By having the courage to reprogram or take another path to break the chains of the traumatic curses takes great faith, trust, and strength. I, with my ancestors' guidance, chose my mom and dad. All of us deal with limiting beliefs like not being good enough or worthy enough to live fulfilling lives. Everyone can live a life full of abundance if we allow it. Unresolved issues or trauma lead to abuse, poverty, or a scarcity mindset where you feel like there will never be enough money, food, clothes, or possessions. People in this mindset may overeat, become hoarders, or do other things to extremes to fulfill the feeling that they may run out. Emotionally the body manifests these as anxiety or depression, amongst other ailments like a rash or suddenly having your leg be sore to the point where it is debilitating. Being able to understand your body, for example, when you are nervous and you get butterflies in your stomach; is your body telling you to take a step back and think twice about what is going on? How does this feel different from when your stomach is rested and calm? I learned that my body is my compass, and by being able to trust myself, and my intuition, I was able to develop my self-worth. It was time to put a stop to all the trauma and heal my family so that future generations could live a more fulfilling life. I committed to taking the steps necessary to break these limiting beliefs at all costs.

Every family has a unique story and has had their unique challenges. The way these challenges were met, solved, and activated a different road for each family story makes each of us uniquely different. People, like my paternal family, immigrated to different areas and countries to make the road easier. As with others, my maternal family's ancestral and generational limiting beliefs were very strong, yet subtle, which made them hard to recognize. In my family, stories were told from generation to generation with the best intentions. Having aboriginal DNA, my Metis ancestors passed on their knowledge, successes, and challenges of establishing themselves in Canada. My paternal side was unknown to me until very recently. My maternal ancestors came from Europe and Quebec, and many were already settled in Canada as the native peoples of the land. I will not get into that part now because that is a whole other series of literature to read.

People around me loved me unconditionally, in their own way. They were carrying all the ancestral baggage as well without realizing it. Trauma can be complex. You don't have to live as a victim. You always have a choice. Like an onion, once the layers are pulled back, you will see that everyone is born with good intentions. Due to societal pressures, family, or friends, many people become robots and end up in victim or survival mode. This was the case for most of my family. It is easier just to survive or blame others than do the hard work required for generational healing for the family.

I chose to love myself, my family, and everything that came with my journey. I learned to explore the deep roots that were my ancestors, Metis and European. I explored and empathized with those around me as I learned to navigate the waters that were part of my journey. The challenges gave me strength. I didn't appreciate them at the time because I didn't understand why all these bad things were happening to me. My mom always said, "God will only give you as much as he knows you can handle." Well, being in a victim mindset for too long, I had enough and decided to change my course, which in turn changed future generations and those around me. Challenges taught me to become innovative and creative. I learned that only I could take the necessary actions to remove the obstacles to become more resilient. I knew I was meant to do so much more than survive, as my ancestors did. I decided to thrive and break the chains that held my family down once and for all!

I am grateful for the challenges presented to me so that I could grow stronger with each one. I forgive all those who feel that they held me back as they worked through their challenges. I understand the difficulties associated with each situation because I have been there. When a person is overwhelmed with a situation, it can be extremely difficult to see that there is always a choice. All else is blurred until the road becomes clear. This is the value that I have learned by becoming a Certified Coach and is what I bring to my clients. True empowerment starts by believing in yourself, one step at a time. I love that I am a multi-faceted being who can relate to many people. This allows me to serve men and women from my heart with love. Let's get started at the beginning.

CHAPTER 2

Empathizing with My World

As an infant, the only person I could rely on at the time was my mom. She was separated from an alcoholic husband at the time (my older sibling's father) and a recipient of our welfare system when she met my dad. My mom and dad were together for about a year and a half, which was long enough to bring me into this world with an abundance of challenges right off the hop! Both families, being of Roman Catholic and French descent, believed that divorce, wedlock, and even sex outside of marriage was a sin and Hell was a real thing. This began the many hypocrisies that were present throughout history. These people were judged and belittled for their shortcomings, and my creators were no different. Repentance was necessary as guilt and judgement were found everywhere. The societal pressures were a huge load to bear for many people. My parents did the best they could with what was presented to them.

My mom knew immediately that she did not want to give me up for adoption for a good reason. This unconditional love provided her with strength that she was not aware she had. The stresses and strain from daily life were passed on to me unintentionally while I grew inside of her. The daily reminder of her feeling that she was "not good enough" was very real. In the 1970s, little was spoken about mental health. Depending on how liberated your family was, blinders were high, and tunnel vision was easier than accepting the harsh realities of healing. In survival mode, the victim mentality developed strongly. I have never been an "easy" child, starting from my birth. I came into this world breech, ass end first. As a young adult and accepting the challenges that I already had, I would joke with her how this was my way of telling those who did not believe in me to "kiss my ass" because I did not need their acceptance, validation, or confirmation that whatever I was doing was right or wrong. I did things the way I felt was right, and if it wasn't, I would learn. The doctors needed to remove me from her uterus via forceps, leaving a birthmark above my belly button that looks like a question mark. I would jokingly say that God, the Universe, Allah …whoever, was unsure about this human. Mom knew differently.

The trust my mother had in me was immense. So much so that she confided deep secrets in me when she felt backed into a corner and had no one she could really talk to. While caring for me, she would talk about whatever she needed to get off her chest. Little did she realize that her burden was now mine. Along with the transfer of DNA, my story of what really happened during the relationship with my dad was being told to me in one way or another. This is where tantric meditations and guidance have taught me exactly who I am, how it is okay to believe in myself, and that my mother did the best she could with what she had.

Financial restrictions were real. My eldest sister, who was three years older, stayed with my grandparents often so that my mom could work as a nurse's aid, or candy striper as they were called in the day. Food banks and help from the church at Christmas cemented the victim mindset further. My mom was told by her parents with crystal clarity, "You made your bed, now lie in it." Help from family was limited while they watched my mom try to figure out life with a grade-seven education. Limited life experience due to the religious blinders that she was raised with was a constant challenge. In my family, many topics that were deemed embarrassing like menstruation, having sexual relations with those you were not sworn to by marriage, or behaviors that could tarnish the family's reputation were not discussed, and sensitive topics were expected to be learned independently. Today the term generational limiting beliefs is more common, though back then, these more aggressive parenting strategies became more traumatic as another generation was created. It was like the past generation lovingly tried to guide the new generation, though this lack of clarity and specificity of direction was denied as raising children became more complicated. Therefore, my mother's unwed pregnancy to someone else while married to another is added to the next generation and repeats itself if there are no actions to drastically change the pathway. As an adult, I saw these challenges repeat throughout history in many families, which is part of the purpose of this book. I understand the struggles and commend my mom for her strength which was passed on to me. While in this survival mode, she became resourceful in navigating any financial assistance that could ease the strain of trying to raise a family.

Currently separated from her marriage, she had a toddler and now an infant on the way. From my understanding, my mom and dad tried to make things work, but judgement and religious pressures of the time were too much. My parents were not willing to explore the alternate routes that were necessary to break these heavy chains. Mom's focus was on providing my sister and I with the bare necessities of life: food, shelter, and clothing, so that we could become productive citizens of society. Anything else that came our way was a bonus. She tried to make the relationship work with my sister's dad, her husband. However, this lasted only another year before she ended the relationship for good to protect my sister and I from his alcohol abuse. My dad was not emotionally mature to become a father at this point, and he made the decisions he did at the time, which I cannot comment on.

I never met my biological father, though I always felt an unconditional love for him. As a child, I would make up stories about him when friends would ask who my dad was and create what the relationship would have been like for my mom and him, which was part of my survival mode. None of this was told to me, and he was never spoken about. These stories got me through many difficult situations with strangers while I explored my world and tried to make sense of my situation. I know now that they dated for eighteen months and that my dad wanted to be part of my life. The challenges I experienced were necessary to help my future clients understand that we are never alone, even though it feels like it. I can relate to feeling like no one understands who you are because I didn't even know who I was back then. Not talking about situations only made them worse. This is how I felt at the time, totally alone, embarrassed, and having no one around me who understood because everyone had a father figure. This is part of the victim mindset I was raised with. A large part felt like I was the only one who was lost and didn't know who I was. Luckily, another part of me felt like I was making the best out of the situation because I knew better things would come! I kept reminding myself that this part of my life was temporary, and I just needed to "get through it!"

I came into this world unexpectedly. Mom did not allow my dad's family the opportunity to be in my life. I understand she was trying to protect me, but this affected me so much more than I understood at the time. It is unclear exactly what the story is regarding my dad, though I have always enjoyed large families and welcomed new family members with open arms. Through my tantric healing, I can remember that he was in the hospital room after my birth to hold me once. Only long enough to build a bond that would last a lifetime as he cradled me lovingly. This was the love that I did not receive growing up. The physical affection where there was no guessing that I was loved, wanted, and belonged to him and I was part of his family, the Aguesse family, which came from Deerhorn, Manitoba. My grandmother, Marie Therese Gantois, came from a small village in Fontenoy le Chateau, Vosges, France. My grandfather was Alexis Aguesse, also from France, though I am still searching for more family. I look forward to the day when I can welcome my dad's family properly. I will discuss this further in a proper sequence of events.

My mom remembers this part differently because this is part of the stories she has made up to survive. The beauty and very difficult part of tantric work is accepting the reality of who you are in black and white, with no blinders on. My mom was not aware of this healing modality, and she stayed in survival mode. Her part of the story is that my maternal grandparents and the priest were in the room when I was born, ready to take me away and put me up for adoption. My mom knew I was meant to be with her, to help her along her journey. Of course, I was one of the biggest challenges of her life, though it brings me solace knowing that she did love me enough to keep me regardless of the uphill battle she would face.

My mom was stronger back then, so she tried to make things work with my older sibling's father, her first real love. This was most likely encouraged by my maternal grandparents. For my mom and her first husband, I felt like I represented the reality of another mouth to feed and care for when life was already difficult for them. They were trying to "work things out." There were no hugs, reading of bedtime stories, no hand to hold, no "I love you," any kind of emotional attachment that could help me navigate these extremely cold waters that were my reality. The grandparents of my older sister would allow me to visit occasionally, but they were not biological. I remember them being very welcoming of me. This grandmother welcomed me as one of her own grandchildren. She made me a brown teddy bear that was made with love, which I still have today. This love was lacking in my daily life, and at the time, it was a reminder that seemed to be everywhere. I was not breastfed, played with, or nurtured with any sort of emotion. These actions would have been crucial and could have helped form some kind of attachment to my mother in my early development. My reality did not involve my biological dad. I came up with two explanations. Either my mom did not want him in my life, or due to the religious upbringing and judgement placed on her by my grandparents, she was told that she had to try to make things work with my eldest sister's dad. I may never know, though I am confident that this was the ultimatum so she did not shame the family.

I am grateful that Mom had the faith in herself to keep me, as it only made our relationship stronger. I forgive her for not telling me the true story about my dad when I needed to hear it. I forgive my dad for not being the man I needed in my life as a role model and parent. I am grateful for my mom's sacrifice of her life to protect me. I am grateful for the ancestry groups and family members I have connected with on my paternal side so my search can continue.

CHAPTER 3

Learning How to Navigate the Waters of Life

Perfectionism was very prominent in my mom's family to make up for low self-esteem. Physically, I was not accepted for who I was. For example, my left eye wandered slightly, so my mother agreed to surgically correct it. I was born "bull-legged" so at age two or three the doctor prescribed brown leather boots that were attached to a very heavy brass bar that I had to walk with and sleep with. I am not sure how long I wore them. All I remember is trying to turn over in bed was quite a challenge- forget using blankets! I remember my mom trying to put me in bed for my nap. This was a challenge because the metal bar was so heavy I could barely lift it, neither of us are very graceful. She would attempt to lift me while I tried to climb into bed. These modifications were so minor that, most likely, I did not "need" correction. They were what made me uniquely me, and this was not good enough for the person who brought me into this world and was supposed to protect me. She allowed others to modify her creation rather than accepting me for who I was. I understand she was listening to what the doctors told her, but they are only human. There are phases in the medical world that seem to be like fads. As the field evolves, the doctors put their newly acquired (and tested in labs) knowledge to the test on their patients to confirm the theory's validity. This would be like when many people were getting their tonsils removed, as I also experienced. Not everyone necessarily needed to have them removed, though it was done just in case. As time went on, the medical field acquired more expertise in various areas and learned to narrow or widen the criteria for a procedure. This can be applied to everything in life as we learn to become more innovative. At the young age that my mother was, in her early twenties, she did not have the confidence or motherly tendencies to protect me because this was how she was raised. This went on throughout my life, so I had to learn to protect myself and be resourceful. She relied on others to make life decisions for me before I came of age to do so.

I did not need the consistent messages that I received of "not being good enough," though there they were. At Christmas concerts, while students around me would receive hugs and praises for their efforts on stage, I received only criticism. "I couldn't hear you," was always Mom's response. Year after year, rather than inserting a white lie which would have raised my self-esteem, it was pushed down further. I was rarely allowed to express myself creatively, verbally, or as my authentic self because I would "embarrass" the family. I was very energetic, always asking questions and curious about everything around me. My mom was so fearful of my zest for life that she allowed outside judgements to dictate how she raised us, just as her mother had. Pressures were debilitating for her. This was what my mom lived with and unintentionally transferred onto me genetically and verbally before I could speak. The trauma was so great that it got closed away into my memory bank and would not open until I was ready. I am grateful for these challenges because they only made me stronger.

My mom married my stepdad when I was about three years old. He adopted my older sister and I because he quickly realized we were a package deal. In her own way, my mom was not giving up on us. He introduced more control over a situation that could easily turn sideways, which it did on many occasions. Though I believe his intentions were good, this introduced another full set of limiting beliefs from his ancestors and family that I was not expecting. In tantric teachings, the miracle of life allows us to pick who our parents are. This was one of those sideways events which had good intentions but brought other issues to the table that I was not ready for. No one knows what the future will bring.

My stepfather became a huge influence in my life, which I will forever be grateful for. However, his limitations affected me (I did not choose him), and I literally had no control over any decision in my life at this point. Even though I love him for being the dad he didn't have to be to me, a biological daughter has a connection with her father that can never be matched. This evidence was around me when he and my mom produced another daughter into our family. We will talk more about this later. The connection with my stepfather was never meant to be on a spiritual level, though perhaps one day, it could be on a surface level. At least, this is what I believed in my core. Respectfully, I selected two people to bring me into this world, and he was not one of them. I want to emphasize that many people are in survival mode because it is easier to ignore the truths inside of us and live on the surface day by day, rather than deal with the ancestral trauma that is the reality, and he brought a lot of additional issues. This included not allowing my paternal father to have any part of my life. The lies continued so that the people who considered themselves my parents could live with their own fictitious reality. I know now that he had the best intentions, knowing I have always worn my heart on my sleeve and my biological father had a track record of stomping on people who cared about him. Like my mom, he did not have the confidence to be the dad I needed at that point. It was easier to keep him out of my life than to deal with the unknown potential consequences, which was one of the limiting beliefs that he brought into my life.

My stepdad brought the security and structure that we all needed in our lives. When I say structure, I mean that term very loosely. Basically, he would go away to work, and when he came home, mom made sure dinner was ready and my older sister and I had to make sure the house was clean. To be honest, the times when he was away are still a blur. We had a small house, but it was all we needed. We each had our own rooms, and my stepdad was good at working with tools. He turned the basement into a rec room/play area for us and a small workshop area for himself. He loved fishing, camping, and many outdoor activities, which was great for a hyper child. When he went fishing, he would proudly string up all the fish in his workshop and smoke them. Mom would get so mad at the smell coming upstairs through the vents, but I thought it was neat. Kind of like Christmas decorations, except they were dead fish strung everywhere in his workshop. He introduced me to many things that I am not sure I would have been exposed to if my mom had not married him.

Between the ages of five to nine, other than the lies about my paternity, life was good for the most part. When we went camping, I learned many life skills. I learned how to mark my path on a trail, use the sunset and sunrise to know what time it was, tell apart good versus bad berries, identify poison ivy, and generally learned how to be okay on my own. My stepfather taught me many life skills in the wilderness about animals and how to protect myself. One outing we enjoyed as kids was going to the garbage dump to see the bears. This was always exciting. He always made sure we stayed in the car as the bears would rummage through the garbage to find treasures. One time after we came home from the dump it smelled really badly of a skunk that sprayed. It turned out that my mom, being slightly innovative herself, found the skunk in the garbage can outside of the camper and sprayed it back with insect repellent. It worked and the skunk met its match that day! I watched how other families and people behaved, and then I would decide whether I thought this was normal or not. I loved being outside. Mother Nature allowed me to explore my world in a different and much gentler way than when we were at home. While camping, we had chores to do, like piling wood after it was split up for firewood, though we were mainly on our own. We would return to the campsite to eat, and then I was off again. This independence brought a lot of responsibility as well, though I guess my parents knew I could handle it, and it also gave them a break from my older sister and I.

Our home on Sheppard Street is where our little unique family lived. This is where all the questions started for me about my dad. My eldest sister had hers, and now my younger sibling had hers, where was mine? Once my younger sibling was born, there was a lot of confusion! I started rebelling in my own way. I got caught stealing a package of Hubba Bubba at Shoppers Drug Mart on Main and Redwood near Mosienko bowling lanes, where my eldest sibling and I were in a Saturday bowling league. This Saturday, Mom was recuperating from having sinus surgery. Arrangements were made to have us picked up by our neighbor. I remember my sister encouraging me to snatch the gum. Being the naïve younger sibling, I trusted everything she said. The shoplifting incident left a huge scar on me. I was told by the police officer that if I didn't change my ways, it would affect my future, and for me at the time, this meant becoming a schoolteacher. School was a hard place for me, so I am not sure why I had it set in my mind that this would be my career. All I knew is that whatever I decided to do, it would end due to my thievery.

I felt ashamed, embarrassed and alone. No one was there to sit with me and tell me everything would be okay, to "please do not do it again because we love you and we are trying our best in this odd situation." To be honest, if someone had said something like that to me, things may have been a whole lot easier. I had no idea where my accomplice went; I barely remember that ride home. The whole incident happened in the time it took for our ride to be there to pick us up, about twenty minutes. I remember thinking I wanted it over so that no one would know; everything would be as it was before, and this lesson would stay with me for life. When the neighbor dropped us off, I was scared to go home, thinking for sure I would get a spanking. I knew the police had called home to tell them what a bad thing I did. I decided to sneak away as soon as the car stopped to go for a walk, all day… until it got dark.

I needed to figure out some things. I was alone and okay with this alone time because I always had been alone, in my head and heart. No one understood or even tried to understand my perspective of what it felt like not having a dad. I remember my stomach being in so many knots that I wasn't hungry. As the streetlights came on, I knew I had to go home eventually and face the wrath that awaited me. I quickly snuck in the door and was able to get to my bedroom. I sat there on my bed wondering if anyone noticed me come in and, if they did, when they would enter to serve my death sentence. It seemed like forever. Finally, my stepdad came into my room and sat on the bed beside me. I was shocked to hear they were worried and glad I was home safely. Then came the guilt that the police were out looking for me, and he was at home taking care of mom because she had surgery that day and was in bed recovering. I added unnecessary worry to an already busy day. How was I supposed to know she was getting surgery? I didn't remember anyone telling me anything about a hospital and surgery. Would that have changed things? Maybe, but probably not. Perhaps I was being selfish? This ran through my mind often as I would contemplate a situation because it was pounded into my head that "there is always someone worse off than you, so be appreciative."

I often felt like a burden that my parents felt obligated to care for because I was not planned and definitely did not feel wanted unless there were chores to do. From a child's perspective, my life had inconvenienced my mother from the start and only provided more problems. I often felt like I would be better off in foster care. My parents telling me to always be appreciative was understood, and I was, though something never sat right, and I couldn't put my finger on it. It always made me think, on an emotional level, if I do not receive any affection from my parents, then how could this get worse if I am already at the lowest level? Not knowing where I came from. Why wasn't there someone coming to pick me up on the weekends? I vaguely remember one weekend when someone, who I am guessing was my dad, came to the door to see me, but my parents sent him away, and I remember my parents were not happy. Everyone was acting weird, and I was told to go to my room. I did not know who this person was, but I remember thinking he was my dad because I felt it in my heart and he was there for me. This is a very faint memory, and when I think about it as an adult, it makes sense. I know my dad wanted to be in my life, but they would not allow it. The issues with my older sister's dad were very stressful, so the easiest way to avoid a repeat of that situation with me was to never let me see him and pretend that he didn't exist.

My eldest sister was a constant in my life, as much as I knew a constant to be back then. She was trying to figure out her own issues with her biological dad and I liked being her sidekick. Most of the time, she didn't mind because she got to be the better character in her mind. She would pretend to be Batman when I would be Robin, or she would be the Lone Ranger and I would be Tonto. I think lots of siblings did this in the 70s. We had to be creative with our time - parents had enough on their plates without providing us with constant entertainment. We were often paired up, and I would miss her on those weekends. I didn't know where she would go, only that she was often angry when she got home, and I needed to stay out of her way. Our relationship was dicey back then because I got bored easily and tended to be a mischievous child. One time when she returned home, I was especially wanting her attention when she needed some alone time. Being the awesome sidekick that I was, I felt I could cheer her up, so I did not listen when she told me to go away. It was a good thing that I was fast because when she got a grip on you, it was tough to get away, and she was strong! Her bedroom was downstairs, since she was older and required some privacy. I don't remember what I said, but she got so angry that she kicked a hole in the wall, tore off doors to her closet, and slammed the door to her bedroom so hard that it wouldn't close properly. She covered the hole in the hallway with a toy baby carriage. It was like this for a long time before the truth came out. I am grateful for being so quick as I ran up the stairs because I may not be here to tell you this story. Months later, we both ended up getting in trouble because she destroyed property, and I didn't give her space... valuable lesson learned.

I forgive my parents for not being there for me emotionally, and I understand their stories. This was trauma that they carried with them from generations earlier. They did the best they could with what they knew. I am grateful for my stepdad coming into my life when he didn't have to. He added a lot of responsibility to his plate that was not his, and children do not appear with a manual. I love and will be forever grateful for the many challenges and lessons he presented me with. There are too many to count, though all valuable as we continue to challenge each other... with love.

CHAPTER 4

Forgivable Life Lessons

There are certain events in life that I am sure you can remember that you would rather forget. Part of my tantric healing is to resurface all those repressed emotions so that I can become a vibrational match to serve my purpose on Earth while I am here. By serving others to the best of my ability, this vibration eventually will return to the source… me. I tried to dive into my healing on my own via self-help books, but I was very unaware of how deep and complicated it is. This complication comes from the many layers that I was not aware really existed. In order to dive deep into my healing and truly understand it even deeper than a DNA level, I strove to heal and comprehend complex spiritual energies. The weird thing is, that healing doesn't have to be complicated if you allow yourself to believe in not only yourself, but also to trust and fully surrender to the Universe, God, Buddha, Allah, or whoever you put your faith into so that goodness can come to you. I believe in Karma. All past challenges were necessary and valuable to make me the person I am now. Though the struggle was real at the time, I will be forever grateful as I have learned to forgive all those people who have tried to change who I was inside, to my core. Regardless of what happens to you, only YOU can change who you are born as.

I want to take a moment to introduce you to my mom. I did not understand or realize her sacrifice growing up until two things happened. One, I had my own children and two, I dove deep into my healing. It is so easy for us to point our fingers at everyone else rather than looking in the mirror and taking responsibility for our own actions. Even though my mom is not the emotional, hip or fashionable mom, she is what I needed. What she isn't is superficial - she is strong willed and determined to survive from her own journey. This rock of a woman would give the shirt off her back to anyone if she could to help them (especially if you are a kitten) because she understands the struggle and resilience that it takes to thrive. She may not have the words to articulate what she feels or sees, though she is wise and knew what she had to do to keep my sister and I safe. Her sacrifice is her love. This is easy to overlook because it is not obvious. While she attempts to speak to anyone, she gladly sits in the back and watches. She could not give out hugs, kisses, emotional support, or fashion advice. She is one of the most authentic people I know! What she provides is worth so much more. She is not aware, though, that she was the brick wall that needed to be held up for me to be taking the journey I am. I could not have done it without her. She knew distinctly what she had to do, and in her own little ways to show she loved us.

I have always been distinctly different from my siblings, and it was almost like she acknowledged the hardship I was going through internally even if she was unable to express empathy. An example of this would be at Easter as children. For many years the Easter bunny would bring us baskets full of low-quality chocolate, candies, and jellybeans that I didn't really like. I don't have a sweet tooth, though I like quality. Those inexpensive bunnies tasted like plastic to me so I would usually take a few bites then give them to my sisters. My mom knew that I preferred Laura Secord chocolate truffles. I was more than content to receive one large truffle from Laura Secord (now from Godiva) than the whole basket of goodies. My siblings would gobble up their treats while I quietly and very contentedly would savour the chocolate, especially the smooth inside. *Mmmmm*, I can still taste it. This is a fond memory of how my mom tried to be supportive. Like I said, it was in her own way. I guess this is like what she says about me and how I am determined to do things my way. She influenced me perhaps more than I initially realized so I acknowledge her here. Thanks Mom!!

There were few toys growing up on a farm, and she learned what she could rely on: animals. Cats are her thing. Almost everyday she has a cat around her in some way, whether it is the shirt she is wearing, a piece of jewelry somehow representing a cat, or pictures of her beloved kitties on her phone. They are great listeners and were always there for her when she needed them. As a girl, while most would have a baby doll in a toy carriage, mom had kittens. Her connection was easier with animals. She speaks their language. After I had my first child at twenty-four years old, I started to understand her in a different way. I wrote her a letter as her Christmas present which apologized for all the unappreciative, unsympathetic things I had done or said growing up. This was the first time I had ever seen a tear. Only one. Then she said, "finally, it's about time" and "thank you." Her vocabulary is not vast, though she gets her point across. These few moments are worth so much more than many of them.

I was a good child, though my questions would often not come out as eloquently as I hoped and were seen as confrontational. I needed to know why things were the way they were, and my curiosity often got me into trouble. I did not grow up with my biological dad or his family. I had to rely on my maternal family. He, and truthfully the situation between him and my mom, was always the elephant in the room that I and everyone around me was not allowed to talk about. I spent a lot of time with my maternal grandparents. My grandfather, Pépère, was very close to me, and I liked this because at least I knew he was my biological grandfather, not someone else's that was being kind to me because they felt sorry for me.

I was always aware that I did not belong in my stepdad's family. At a young age I could feel the conditional love and support that came with forced intention of nurturing. I saw evidence of it in families all around me. I longed for real affection that I was denied by my parents. I spent a lot of time with Pépère as he taught me about gardening, woodworking, fixing little trinkets, and basic yard work tricks that helped to get the jobs done more efficiently. He would make us wooden toys, and my younger sister and I received a doll house to share. She and her dolls could live on one side and I on the other, with a door in the middle so we could visit. My eldest sister and I each got a cedar hope chest where our most prized possessions were kept. I deeply loved spending time with my grandfather not only because we had fun and played together, but because he took the time to teach me how to be more resourceful in different environments so that I could survive the place that I had to call home. Knowing our biological connection made this relationship even stronger for me. I had always been aware of this and would often study family members' faces and mannerisms, wondering what I inherited from Dad's side. Little did my grandfather realize, I studied what he taught.

Pépère had a shop in the basement where he would build my siblings and I our handcrafted toys and fix or build things for family members. This was his happy place. The beauty of everything he did and built came from the intention and love he put into his projects. He modelled the importance of consistent learning for growth. In his workshop he had the main area where he did his work, and there was also an area kind of hidden and off to the side that could be easily missed. He kept all the various types of wood neatly piled and sorted waiting for the next project. He had a very vivid imagination that he brought to many inanimate objects. The layout of the basement will always be embedded in my mind. He had his workshop while my grandmother, Mémère, had a sewing area, and they would reserve an area for the numerous plants for vegetable gardening that would turn into canning under the basement stairs. I was always allowed to go wherever I wanted in the house, even Pépère's area, until one day I wasn't.

Being the curious 8-year-old that I was, I was looking for something in a drawer in his workshop and found some magazines of very scantily dressed women that were very different from the magazines that my grandmother read. I asked my grandmother about the magazines to which she claimed she knew nothing about them and that I should just ignore them. I told my mother because I did not understand, and something didn't feel right. My intuition was telling me that there was something wrong about this situation. At a young age I wanted to ensure that everyone was okay emotionally and physically. My mom denied this and claimed that I didn't see things right. I remember going back to look for them and they were gone. They had been moved because I knew what I saw, and my mind was seeing things correctly. My grandfather was looking at dirty magazines and not telling anyone. I know now that everyone probably knew, especially my grandmother. My Catholic upbringing told me that this was a sin, so what was wrong with Pépère that he would degrade himself to this level? I would not realize these answers until decades later.

Mom was driving my sister and I to Brownies and Girl Guides when I casually brought it up because this is what I did. We had a station wagon at the time and seatbelts were not mandatory. Sitting in the back, I casually leaned over to the middle of the front seat and told my mother what I found. Without skipping a beat, because my mother had been well trained by my grandmother (and generations before them), she would not help with clarification on the matter and, honestly, I really should have minded my own business. Rather than explaining that some things are private and that I shouldn't be snooping around, her secrecy only made my curiosity worse. I was not allowed to explore or talk about anything personal or sexual, and they made it seem as if it was a mountainous secret that the rest of the world was not allowed to know about, so I bottled it up. She said that my "mind is playing tricks on me" and that I "didn't see what I thought I saw." This was common as I tried to piece things together. This became another "elephant in the room" situation that I was learning was the norm for our family. I was ten years old when the sexual abuse started.

According to the Oxford Legal Dictionary, child abuse is defined as "…any kind of sexual activity with a minor." This includes "when an adult fondles, or touches a minor, speaks obscenely to a minor, exposes themselves to a minor, produces naked images of a minor," and so on. This article includes a description of the abuse of power and refers to the "Stop Abuse Campaign, an ACE study defines emotional abuse as a parent or other adult in the household often swearing at you, insulting you, putting you down, humiliating you, or acting in a way that made you afraid that you might be physically hurt. It's important to notice the word 'often' here; a single instance of parental bad behavior is not enough to cause a lifetime of trauma for children." (www.oxfordlegal.com, "Oxford Legal; Legal Definitions," June 13, 2021, Gabriel Taylor). It is necessary to include this definition very directly and intentionally into my book because this was my childhood. Too many people minimize what has happened to them. In my case, I include this portion to help bring awareness of the severity of abuse. In my opinion, people often ignore the signs because the reality of deep, emotional trauma is too hard. I thought my grandfather was being affectionate. Having been raised without any sort of emotional affection, I thought someone in this cold family finally realized how badly I craved to be loved.

My family moved to Whitemouth and the abuse only got worse. I was so confused. This was someone I loved, trusted, and respected unconditionally. Why was this happening to me, and especially by him? What did I do wrong to deserve this? When I realized what was happening and how wrong it was, I knew that in order to survive I had to start thinking outside the box. Learning to become resourceful became the norm for my survival. I could not count on anyone but myself. Both my mother and grandmother had not been supportive when I found the magazines, they definitely would not be now! This internal struggle was emotionally and mentally draining. I did not want to admit just how bad the trauma in my family was. In the early eighties, the word abuse alone would make heads turn! I started to create my own reality and tried to form a new identity. I was able to dodge the sexual abuse at fifteen years old by purposely not being around when my grandparents would visit. Having what I considered to be a "normal family next door" became my hideaway. Sometimes my grandparents would arrive without notice. I got very good at making up my own stories that I had to be somewhere else. I had to physically leave the building because he would follow me and lock the door behind him. My neighbour's daughter became my best friend partly because of the good role models that her family portrayed, but I was able to "hide out" until I thought my grandparents were gone. They did not know the reality of what was happening next door. I started pushing all those vulnerable feelings down because they did not feel good. I was beyond embarrassed that my family was so dysfunctional. I showed that I was not like my parents by striving to achieve whatever I could for attention. I had some good ideas like getting ribbons in 4-H rallies and other desperate cries for help, such as faking sprained wrists 3-4 times, and going to the hospital when I lived in Whitemouth just so I would get attention from the town doctors thinking, "They're doctors, surely they would help me out?" I was wrong. They would wrap me up and send me on my way. Surely, they knew that I was craving attention? So, whether they said something to my parents or not, nothing came from it. I had to be stronger and I vowed to never put myself in a vulnerable situation again if I could avoid it.

As a teenager I learnt exactly who I did not want to become. The people who were supposed to protect me - my parents, grandparents, and immediate family. My stepdad tried hard to provide everything I needed as a child; food, shelter, clothing, and activities to teach us about nature, work ethic, and enjoying the simple things in life like driving around at Christmas time to see the lights. However, he would never fill the void of my biological father or the emotional connection that I could only feel when I had my children. I will be forever grateful because I know he did the best that he could with what he was given by his ancestors. He did not have to adopt my sister and I as his own, but this was a condition placed on my mom that she accepted because she was not strong enough to raise us on her own. I want to remind the reader of the context because my parents were victims of their environments, just as generations before them were. Think of all the wars, depressions, financial hardships, lack of technology, and countless other examples in history that made us who we are. We can either accept who we are OR truly look in the mirror and figure out how we can do better for ourselves and others. The generationally limiting beliefs were at full force as a teenager, and I allowed that black hole in my chest to get bigger.

As a child, I thought that my younger sister got special treatment, though as an adult and mother I know differently. She was the biological offspring of my stepdad, this is true, though she has her own unique story, and this is not my place to tell it. I respect the journey that she has had and is on because it makes her special and I love her for it. She presents her own strength in her own way, just like my mom. The truth is that our parents were not present emotionally, physically, or mentally for 85% of our lives. If I would have been writing this thirty years ago, this chapter would have been very different. There was a lot of jealousy, anger, and resentment on my part towards my younger step sister because not only did she know who her mother and father were, she had a relationship with them. Was allowing myself to feel these emotions fair of me? Of course not. I was stuck in the victim mentality and being a martyr was easier than taking that hard look in the mirror. The emotions I was feeling were very raw, and I did not know how to acknowledge or process them. My parents put a lot of responsibility on my shoulders for her care.

One day I exploded. I was about thirteen and I destroyed her side of the bedroom that we shared. I turned her bed upside-down, shelves were cleared with a swoop of an arm, and laundry and toys were everywhere. It was not a pretty scene. Thank goodness she was not around. This tantrum was necessary for me to make any kind of sense of the abuse and abandonment that was occurring in my world. She was about six or seven, and I could no longer handle picking up after her, ensuring lunches were made, singing her to sleep, reading to her, helping with homework, bathing, getting to bed, and getting her to school. These were basic parenting things that I wanted help and attention with. For me, everything seemed conditional, and she had none of these conditions placed on her because she existed. I felt I always had to prove myself, while she didn't. True healing for me did not happen until I was in my forties. In my twenties and thirties, I sacrificed my healing and myself for my children because they were my priority. Taking responsibility for my actions and reactions were valuable lessons. I did help her clean up her room and apologised for the mess I had made.

My parents made me responsible for taking care of a six-year-old girl at twelve years old. This was how children were raised in many families historically, especially on farms. Older siblings reared younger ones so that parents could provide the necessities of food, clothes, and shelter. We are six years apart and shared a room for about seven years. Being able to understand the trauma that I was dealing with made it easier to heal and forgive myself of any acts I felt were harsh at the time. She had to process similar traumas due to our parents' lack of healing for themselves. I realize that this sounds terrible, and I will make no excuses, nor will I play the victim. Our parents thought that buying us gifts and providing us with the necessities was enough. Mental health was not as known, discussed, or effectively handled in the seventies. I accept this and know differently now.

I would love to say that I tried to protect her from the harsh, cold realities that were our family, but this would be a lie. For many years I held a lot of disdain towards her. I was going through so many feelings that I didn't understand how I was supposed to help her. This is like what our parents were going through, but were unaware of the consequences that their actions played in our lives. I was so confused about the way Pépère was acting, so I tried to stay away from home as much as possible.

As children, what we experienced then would be defined as abandonment today. No wonder I grew up naively thinking I was invincible. The only regular meal was Sunday dinner. The rest of the week I had to make all my meals myself, which included using a grill and a deep fryer. This was not safe for a ten-year-old girl. Luckily there were employees who worked for my parents who looked out for us. They treated us like their family. Never my parents, just us kids. Everyone probably saw this lack of love and ability to be real parents. We came home when the streetlights came on. As long as our chores were done, we fended for ourselves; my parents were preoccupied with running the hotel. Let's call out this elephant right now. My stepdad enjoyed the attention he got by being a hotel owner. He would buy rounds of drinks, winning over patrons and regular customers. Yes, they put in their time maintaining the general operations of the business, and this did require a lot of commitment, but so does raising children. My mom was following my stepdad's lead, and he was doing what he thought was best for the business because it provided an income for the family.

When my cousins heard that we had a hotel, they thought it was amazing. I thought, "if you only knew." As an adult it is clear that it is a terrible place to raise a young family, in my opinion. In the beginning it seemed like heaven. I could eat whatever I wanted, go to bed later than I normally would, and had quite a bit of freedom. My parents were always so busy trying to operate the functioning of the hotel that my siblings and I were one of the last things they were worried about. All our lives literally got turned upside down. My stepdad now had even more on his plate because my mom was not skilled at any sort of bookwork or day end procedures. As children, we were fortunate that the hotel employed wonderful maternal figures who cooked in the restaurant. They ensured my sisters and I got fed, and I can remember a few times that we were invited over to their homes for a home cooked meal. One lady had children the same ages as us and there was only one school in town, so we would hang out occasionally. I remember cooking my own meals which included using a deep fryer and industrial grill at the age of eleven or twelve. One Saturday, my older sister was supposed to start working in the kitchen at the age of fifteen. She was lighting the gas deep fryer and she didn't do something correctly. She burnt both of her eyebrows off which, to this day, have never grown back. Working in the hotel taught me work ethic and how to navigate adult waters in a child's body.

In the end, I forgave my parents because they did not know what they didn't know, and this is what healing does. Instead, I will tell you some of the benefits that the hotel provided for us. It did allow us to view MTV's latest music video before anyone else in town got to see it. We had the only satellite in town back then. We went shopping and ate in restaurants more than we ever had while living in the city. There were many interesting chores that we had while living in a hotel. My eldest sister and I bagged ice that people purchased for get-togethers. We received ten cents per bag and were happy with it because we could go to the local sundries store and buy a TeenBeat Magazine or some candies. We vacuumed the bar on Sundays (eager to find any change that might have dropped on the floor), swept and washed the floors in the restaurant, and helped clean the hotel rooms. Cleaning the rooms was like a right of passage for when we gained enough experience after bussing tables and being janitors. These jobs are required to be done with a certain amount of professionalism. Learning to make those hospital corners thrilled me. Everything was done with such intention. This was very different from what I was used to from my mother.

CHAPTER 5

The Many Parts of Me
(Undiagnosed ADHD)

*"I am not what I think I am. And I am not what you
think I am. I am what I think you think I am."*
— Jay Shetty *Think Like a Monk*

As I got older, total confusion reigned to the point where it was easier to numb myself with alcohol than deal with feelings. As a child, I tried to make sense of who I was and what story I wanted to make up for myself so that I would feel like I belonged somewhere. I knew very clearly that my family was keeping things from me, and I obviously wasn't going to get a straight answer. I tried to rationalize my situation by looking at the families around me. One friend would go see her dad on weekends, but she lived with her mom full-time. Another friend had both his mom and dad who he lived with, and this is what I was told was the "proper" way for a family to be. There was another girl I hung out with occasionally and she only lived with her mom as well. She was mean though, so I didn't go there often. I understood many years later that her being mean was a similar situation to my older sister; she had lots of anger and did not know how to process the emotions she was feeling. Being involved in organized activities and sports kept me off the streets and at least my parents would know where I was. Around the age of seven, I started Brownies, then Girl Guides, and I loved swimming lessons. These all taught me very important life lessons and basic survival skills which I was keen to learn. I seemed to subconsciously know that the more skills I acquired, the more prepared I would be for when I was out on my own. As a young teenager I was encouraged to join Air Cadets, and I started delivering newspapers. Many of these skills my stepdad did to prepare me for adulthood and to be a responsible citizen. I truly believe in Karma and that the universe always has my back because many people were brought into my life who I needed. Without the truth of who my father was and my mother allowing everyone else to make decisions about what would be best for me, I am grateful I turned out the way I did.

Not knowing the truth about who I was made it much more difficult than my parents will ever understand. I tried to stay away from home as much as I could, hoping that maybe that man who came to the door once when we lived in Winnipeg would come back for me. Maybe that was my dad? Otherwise, why would my parents have been acting so strangely? I remember thinking that if I stayed outside maybe he would see me, and we would be reunited, and everything would be okay. Like one big happy family. Maybe I watched a little too much Disney or *Little House on the Prairie*. I imagined he would stop the car, talk to me, and I would naturally go with him because he wouldn't feel like a stranger. It would feel natural and meant to be. Thoughts of "don't talk to strangers" and ways that kids were kidnapped and bad things happening to them played in my mind on a regular basis. I thought of running away to find him. I visualized a situation similar to the one at the bowling alley where I would get picked up from the school bus, and rather than going to school, I would just walk away. Sounds easy, right? My common sense (or intuition as I know it now) would kick in and I would rationalize how much worse the situation may be. I also thought, "I have a mixed-up family now and at least they pretty much put up with me, good and bad." What if I wasn't good enough to be part of anyone else's family and this is what I was left with? I decided to stick it out and see how things would play out. At least there was food, shelter, clothes, and my own room with my things. I would stay. As a child, I realized I was very limited at this young age by what I could do on my own. I was not old enough to get a job and I had no money to buy groceries or things I needed. I started to learn to be resourceful by taking some coins out of my mom's wallet. When we moved to a rural community in Whitemouth, Manitoba. Life really changed, and I had to grow up fast. Something I love about myself is the vast array of talents I acquired as I tried to figure myself out. Being a very active child, my parents often told me to "sit still," and "think before you talk." I think they encouraged me to join activities like Air Cadets and 4-H to keep my very active mind occupied. I will go on a brief tangent because this is what I do and is authentically me.

My mother would often lose track of me in stores and referred to be as scatterbrained. One time we went on a family excursion to Grand Forks when I was about eleven or twelve years old. We, my two sisters and parents, went to Columbia Mall, one of the largest malls in the city at that time. I would often see something that interested me and head in that direction. I knew to tell one of the family members where I was going and when to meet them back in the agreed place. I would try not to stray far and tried to keep one of them within eyesight. However, time must have gotten away from me because I could not find my family anywhere. Things were a lot different before cell phones and being a child, I didn't have any money on me. I told a salesperson and they called for my family a few times. I remember feeling embarrassed, scared, and ashamed because I was alone and one of those kids who was now making everyone look at me when they passed by. My family unit literally left the mall without me! I tried to look confident like I was just waiting for someone and all was normal. Inside, I was yelling and tantruming big time. At this point, I really didn't want to know what the onlooking people were thinking. I waited between the entrance doors for at least three hours! No wonder I often felt confused and like

I didn't belong. To this day, no one admits who realized I wasn't in the car first. The part that hurt the most is that my parents were mad that they had to come back for me, and later they made it seem like a joke and blamed me for their irresponsible behavior. It wasn't another town or city, it was another country, and they left me there. I was a child. It was portrayed as "normal" growing up that I was blamed for my parents' lack of parenting skills. I realize now that they did the best they could with what they knew, but many times, especially when I think back as an adult, a bit more common sense would have been nice.

I enjoyed being in organizations like Air Cadets and 4-H so that I could build on the person I was hoping to become one day. At the time, Attention Deficit Hyperactivity Disorder (ADHD) was not a well-known thing. Children were described as difficult to handle or were known as "problem children". That was how I felt and it seemed like no matter what I did my mother always found something to criticize. I decided to be the person that other people wanted me to be so that I would be accepted, and this was never good enough, so I learned skills that I still find value in today. Air Cadets provided me with the structure that I did not have at home. I enjoyed and thrived in this atmosphere because I had never had it. Communication was very clear and I knew exactly *what* I had to do, *when* to do it, was taught *how* to do it, and *why* certain events required extra training. When I participated in 4-H, the lessons were similar. My leaders would take the time to show me patiently how to sew, learn public speaking skills, and how to prepare and lead a group. Both Air Cadets and 4-H taught me the value of being organized and prepared. Learning to serve from my *heart*, doing with my *hands*, thinking and being resourceful with my *head* and ensuring that my *health* was first and foremost (because otherwise the other three would be more difficult). The difference at home was that I would be asked to do something but not shown any of this guidance. It was expected of me to figure it out and if I had trouble figuring it out, I would be criticized and made to feel like an idiot. I received consistent messages from my family that I was not smart enough to figure things out on my own at twelve years old.

When we moved to rural Manitoba, my parents purchased a hotel. This became the excuse for most things as to why my parents could not spend time with us. It was clear that the hotel came first because this was our livelihood now. I became best friends with the girl next door - we were inseparable. Her family showed me how a mom, who was also a business owner of a grocery store, was able to manage working full-time plus manage a household with three children and still find time for herself. She was instrumental during my early teenage years, 11-14 years old, and became a second mom. She did things for her children that I am sure many kids take for granted like having lunches made for them and having a regularly scheduled dinnertime with all family members present. Every meal or lunch involved all food groups and always had homemade desserts, cookies, or muffins. Bedtime was part of the schedule, and I witnessed how each child was read to, cuddled with, given hugs and kisses, and shown how to take care of themselves. They were encouraged to brush their teeth two times a day, wash their face, and make sure their bags were ready for school the next day. These signs of affection were foreign in my world.

Yes, these parenting skills take time and attention which is why she was an awesome mom! I kept these lessons with me and established them when I had a family. She took me to get my first ear piercing, helped with 4-H projects, and was often the driver when we, her daughter and I, needed to go somewhere, like a 4-H Rally. She will always be in my heart as I will be forever grateful for the family providing a safe place for me when things were out of control in my world at home. The stability showed me that I did have skills, and reinforced that I was a person with so much more inside than what I knew thus far. I was able to relax and calm my active, monkey mind at my friend's house, whereas at my house those monkeys were having a party.

Living with undiagnosed, unmedicated ADHD is a very real thing for me. Ask anyone who really knows me - everyday can be an adventure! I was, and still am, interested in many things, and I want to try as much as I can while I am still able to. As a teenager I never thought that I had an issue with staying focused; I am interested in many things. I realize now that it was easier to keep my mind busy than to deal with the realities of the environment I was forced to live in. Jay Shetty defines "the monkey mind as aimless, jumping from thought to thought, and challenge to challenge, without resolving anything," in *Think Like a Monk*. Through my education including Coaching Certification with JSCS (Jay Shetty Certification School) and experiences, I have learned that hyperactivity at the core has two degrees. The first is childhood trauma as you attempt to stabilize the instability that is your life, and the other is that you attempt to make everything perfect, so you will never be satisfied with what you do and turn into someone you are not. My main intention to figure out who I was got lost during my journey as I tried to direct, correct, and take actions that I thought would aid my quest for authenticity. I got very good at repressing my emotions. My maternal grandmother taught me that showing weakness, or your true feelings, was not good and it was better to push down those emotions than allow yourself to be vulnerable or risk getting hurt. This lack of authenticity severely handicapped me for decades.

I am thankful that my ancestors have graced me with many abilities like resourcefulness, determination, and empathy. I forgive them for any challenges that were extreme at the time. I realized that I needed them in order to be able to move forward. I love them for believing in me, protecting me, and driving me to always be better than I was the day before.

CHAPTER 6

Authentically Me

As I tried to grow into the person I did not know yet, I wished to be able to do all the things for my children (and myself) that I never had so that they (and I) would be proud of me. I was very involved in school extracurricular activities as a student myself, then later again when my children were in school. As a child sitting for too long in a classroom was not my thing and as a parent I was able to be part of my children's world in both a social and parental aspect. I enjoyed sports, politics, organizing, and helping wherever I could. Throughout this growth, I needed to figure out a way to heal, grow, and somehow become the best version of myself without bringing the hardship of my family dynamic with me. In my world where until my early teens I had no control of my life, getting involved was a way that I could figure out how to reach a new level of independence where I wouldn't just be surviving. I was learning how to thrive!

Many things that I did were uncommon as I tried to figure out who I was at the core, my truly authentic self. I tended to gravitate towards the underdogs because I could relate to them. One of my authentic truths is that I sucked my finger until I was twelve years old. Am I proud that it took me up until I was twelve years old to break this habit? No, though I have learned to accept that this was a huge part of my story and why I got into the dental field. Over my twenty-three years as a Dental Assistant, I have shared with a limited few the story of why I chose this field. In a nutshell, due to my finger sucking, I developed a severe overjet. This is commonly known as buck teeth. At many ages, kids can be mean and bullying became a common occurrence for me. My nickname in Whitemouth was beaver, then at fifteen years old when we moved to Ste. Agathe I went to school in Morris and the school mascot was a beaver! My initial reaction was, "you have got to be kidding!" I was trying to create a new identity but I guess this was the universe saying that the old me, my true self, is okay too. At least at this point I had already started orthodontic treatment and was on my road to a great future. I felt that I could leave the chaos from Whitemouth behind me and start fresh, though I would be much wiser. I tried to be someone different by doing the things that other kids would not volunteer to do. That is what I have always done. I am always up for a challenge.

Sucking my finger was my first form of security that could not be taken away, and I realized as an adult this was me depending on myself when I felt there was no one else. I found out, 50 years later, the power of words and how they affected me. My mom always told me to ignore the bullies and told me about the rhyme "sticks and stones could break my bones, but words will never hurt me." In all fairness, I think having bones broken occasionally would have been easier than dealing with words that are invisible and affect someone to their core. The importance of what seems to be an insignificant fact of sucking my finger is an example of how unsecure the environment was that I grew up in. The stress that my mom was going through she confided in me because as an infant I could not talk. I have a photo, where I cannot be more than five or six months old sitting in my crib, and I look shit scared! If I could read my thoughts, it would most likely be something like, "What the heck did I get myself into?" This was the reality that I had to accept. I cannot change the past, only the future. I had to learn to suck it up and become the strong, resilient, playful, courageous, empathetic, and determined person I am today. This must have been the image that I had in my mind for myself because intuitively I knew. This is what my tantric healing has taught me, and being of a scientific mindset where there must be a reason for everything, the idea that the universe always has my back is the one that makes sense. I chose for my mom to bring me into this world. It has taken many unanswered wonders throughout my life for me to fully and completely understand and accept my purpose on this Earth.

As a toddler, my mom thought that I was too young to understand what she was saying to me when she would divulge the latest stressors that overwhelmed her as a single parent. What she didn't understand is that communication comes in many forms, and I was much more intelligent than everyone gave me credit for. The frustration, anger, resentment, judgement, loneliness, and utter chaos came through to me loud and clear. Once I entered her womb, the anxiety was mountainous. Her relationship with my dad was full of toxicity, from what she told me. I will not make a comment on this topic because my dad is not here to defend himself. As I got older and started to speak, she could make up stories and I would still believe her, because for whatever reason, I needed to love her. My dad's side of the story stayed hidden from me intentionally. For me, I did not have a dad and my mom was emotionally unstable. She was depressed on and off constantly, hence another underdog scenario. Today this is also known as being stuck in a victim mindset. The scarcity mindset, feeling as if there is never enough. For example over eating because food during the wars, depression, etc. was hard to come by, and you literally did not want to starve to death. She was also dealing with her own life situations, but from our ancestors as well. Having this firsthand experience is why I became a Trauma Awareness Coach.

My mom and my stepdad reformed my real story with untruths to stop me from asking questions and being curious. It was also easier for them to deal with. My mom was not aware of the effect that it was having on me as an infant, toddler, and even as a child. If the lies got her through another day, that was her priority. She was able to take the load off and transfer this burden of truth. People around me did not understand why I did what I did when my parents provided my basic needs of food, shelter, clothes, and some outings. Judgement was all around me. What a spoiled child I must be! Who did I think I was to expect any more than what I received? My mom was caught up in her own story, just surviving while my stepdad was very happy. He had a bouncing baby girl of his own. All I wanted was a brother, and I couldn't even get that! This is an example of the masculine energy that I longed for. We had enough girls in the family. I found out later during my healing journey that this longing was due to the absence of my father. I learned quickly to keep a smile on my face, to not get in the way, and become a sponge for knowledge so that I could become resilient.

When I speak of "family" the family I am referring to is my mom's side. They were around often, especially after we moved to Ste. Agathe. My aunt and uncle lived close by so I would visit often. They became a place to go when home was chaotic. This aunt introduced me to energy work which I am grateful for. I didn't understand the magnitude of this work then, until one Thanksgiving when I was a single parent and after the most recent car accident (of which there were many). I had severe headaches and my shoulders and neck were greatly debilitating my desire to thrive and get through preparing dinner for the family. My aunt strongly encouraged me to sit down and have an open mind as she began treating me with Reiki. I could feel the tingles course through my body as she explained that this was the energy. My neck and shoulders were much more fluid, and my headache was almost gone. This taught me the value of using this natural resource that so many people are unaware of. It took many treatments, though she was able to help me while we were in our own homes. Energy is everywhere! My grandparents would come to visit, though as I explained earlier, I got very good at avoiding them. This was the town that my grandmother grew up in, so my mom felt right at home. It was a regular thing for cousins to start popping out of the woodwork. I will admit that meeting a bit more of my family was interesting at first, but then the thoughts and questions about who my dad was started coming up even more. There were many questions that I needed to have answered. My confidence on this topic was non-existent. If I ever even tried to bring something up, my mom would change the topic abruptly or shut it down quickly. It was very evident that something bad happened, and I would not be getting any information from her.

The institution of learning in general was taken literally for me and I applied this learning to most things I did. I wanted to learn everything I could in order to always be better than the day before. By becoming the high school yearbook editor, I learned to lead a group, prioritize projects, schedule, and accomplish goals by encouraging my team to stay on task and be focused. For me this was huge. I think what made it more achievable was that I was helping others and it was for the common purpose of providing memories and a keepsake for my schoolmates. Being a part of my children's childhood was always a must for me. I wanted them and others to know that they could rely on me. I served on their Parent Auxiliary Council for five years, ending with the presidential role for the last three; I was always part of their sports team's management including hockey, ringette, football, dance, and whatever else they were interested in at the time in many positions including treasurer and fundraising coordinator. I believe in giving back to show gratitude for community clubs that help support the growth of my children's lives. This was a part of me learning to be resourceful. As a single parent, my children would never have been able to participate in the many sports teams, camps, and organizations as they did without the support of the community we were a part of. As a parent, every small act adds up. For example, providing a ride to help bring children to a team practice, game, or event is significant. For myself as a single parent, I will be forever grateful as I could not have done it without these many people. With three children often times would conflict for practices. There were two dads in particular who accepted that my son would need a ride and they coordinated it between the two of them rather than add to my plate. They were amazing communicators between the three of us which was a huge help. The concept of giving back was ingrained into me and I am grateful for this as I know now it to be good Karma. Giving back is always an amazing source of feel-good energy. Gotta love that!

All these experiences contributed to our lives significantly, reinforcing that there are always people to help and provide hope that is essential when dreaming big. Through *The Big Sister Big Brother* organization my daughter was able to go to Disney World for a day! My eldest was paired with the best "Big Brother" for him, which after fifteen years they are still part of each other's lives. I learned how to work with many different personalities on a professional level, giving me the confidence to start becoming more aware of how I could really make a difference in people's lives. When I was younger, I did a lot of volunteering because it was the "right thing to do." I learned that I could help on a slightly bigger scale for a larger community, like the community of Dental Assistants in Manitoba.

I stepped out of my comfort zone again and allowed myself to become vulnerable to colleagues. This was huge for me. I sat on the Board of Directors for six years during which I became an integral part in changing by-laws, consistently reinforced the boards' purpose, and participated in sub-committees in order to make the dental assisting world in Manitoba a better place for all who worked with us. Growing up with my stepfather's influence of rule-following and advocating for change, I was excited about the possibilities that this idea held. I held the roles of secretary and treasurer for most of my terms. Staying true to myself was forgotten as I put all my energy into what was best for the dental assistants. I will admit that I was getting frustrated with the process because I could see things from a different lens, and either no one else wanted to be authentic in our actions or they allowed fear to hold them back from truly taking the actions that needed to be done. After some pivotal events instigated by myself, it became clear that it was time for me to end my term. Titles, recognition, and promotions meant absolutely nothing because I forgot who I was at the core in the process.

My parents' resistance to change was strong and only presented them with more limitations, which in turn only made me stronger. I am grateful for that opportunity. I forgive those who tried to chain me down because it only added fuel to my fire. I send love and strength to those who are allowing guilt, fear, or limiting beliefs hold them back from being their best selves. Everyone was born with a purpose. To stay authentic and passionate to whatever this may be is what makes each of us unique.

Pictures Speak 1000 Words

1971-My Godmother and I. She provided the first portal to discovering my paternity.

At 10 months old I learned to make do and be grateful for what I had. Cold, hard, plastic similar to the emotions shown to me.

Circa 1974- My eldest sister, always looking on to see what I would do next. I definitely kept her on her toes!

I got very good at adapting to whatever the situation was by repressing my true feelings. At this age and time was at the height of the childhood sexual abuse.

I enjoyed the structure that Air Cadets provided during my early teens when everything was chaotic at home. Approximately 13 years old. I was proud of my Corporal stripes. They represented that I was not a "scatterbrain".

14 years old - Confirmation, awkward for so many reasons.

Grade 7- I was embarrassed of my teeth at a young age.
This is rare footage of my 12mm overjet (buckteeth).

My first car, a 1982 Toyota Cressida, just back from a school trip to
France. Right to my paternal roots without realizing it.

First wedding with my eldest child. This new path brought a lot of uncertainty.

First family photo as a single parent and new dental assistant. The look in my eyes shows how I was barely keeping things together on the inside.

Mission trip to Uganda, Africa 2019.

Robin and I with my trusty sidekick Sam.

CHAPTER 7

The Truth Breaks Free

My mom's youngest sibling, who was also my Godmother, is the person I should have paid more attention to for information about my dad. When I was young, she tried to build a relationship with me. My mom ensured that this didn't happen. In words that were told to her, she described herself as the "misfit". The one who never fit in, just like me (both of my siblings had straight blond hair while mine was curly, and auburn). I find it interesting how the childhood rhyme, "sticks and stones may break my bones, but words will never hurt me" was used so often. Physically the damage was not apparent, though inside the wounds were deep. She grew into the "misfit" that people labelled her as. My mom and the aunt who lived near us were very mean to her, and I saw this growing up. The belittling, judgement, shame, and embarrassment that those around her felt was due to their fear of their own demons. My aunt was a kind soul and tried to help who she could with what she had. She had very little, but she was always willing to share with the ones who accepted her for who she was. I wish that I had been more kind to her because I know there was more that I could have learned. I used to make the excuse that she and I didn't have anything in common. Now I see that we had a lot more in common than I cared to admit. She also grew up with no emotional support and had to learn to be resilient. My grandmother would help her financially, and her siblings would ridicule her even more for this. I believe my grandmother realized the mistakes she had made raising her children and tried to make things right by providing financial aid. On the other hand, my aunt helped everyone around her with love and compassion, sacrificing herself.

Her eldest son, my cousin, and I are only a few months apart and I enjoyed going to visit. I remember my aunt being the person that you could talk to about anything; life, sex, and I realized too late, my dad (which is why my mom kept us apart). My mom put an end to this in fear that I would find out the truth about my dad or whatever other secrets she harboured. I can remember at times when my mom would tell her that she was saying too much. Our relationship really started to fade after we moved away from the city. It felt almost as if by moving rurally, my mom and stepdad were running away from the truth that seemed to lie in the city. They did not want to deal with these issues, so by running away they could avoid them along with any other truly important facts about my life. My aunt held many of the secrets which would have brought us closer together. I am guessing that the visits stopped because she was a "bad influence" on me in the eyes of my parents. I can see how my aunt was attempting to break the limiting familial beliefs by telling the secrets that needed to be told. I can only imagine the pressures that she had holding her back. Members of the family rarely had anything good to say about her which made me sad. I will remember her fun spirit and attempts at fighting for what she believed in. Lack of education during her life made it so she didn't have enough resources to make bigger changes. She always did what she could with what she had. When she passed away in 2020, even her burial represented the true isolation she must have felt from the family. I send her love and compassion for herself as she deserved. She can be at peace now.

I feel the last gift that my aunt gave me was when I was nineteen years old. She came for a visit and opened the door to my world just a smidge. We were sitting in the bar (I was of legal serving age now) and she matter of factly stated that my biological father was dead. Just like that. This is an example of the things my mother tried to "protect" me from. My aunt would say things either not realizing the importance of the entire story, or she would distort the information. It was a good thing that I was sitting down because I nearly fell over! I questioned her right away asking if she was sure. She said yes because she saw it in the paper and showed it to me, but I could not focus. She did not specify the obituaries, just the paper (I found the article years later in the Winnipeg Free Press that he was severely beaten and left to die in his home for 4 days until someone found him. He became paralyzed on the entire left side of his body and he remained in a care home until he passed on July 23, 2008). I was in shock not only because it was about my dad, but the unspoken name was used for the first time ever: Ted (Theodore) Aguesse. Until that point, I never even knew his name. When I was younger, I used to make up stories and tell people that his name was Joe. My middle name is Joanne, so I put "Joe" (signifying my dad) and my mom's name "Anne" together. As I quickly processed this I thought, "I have a name, but he may be dead…great. Still, I will take these two pieces of the puzzle. Thank you, Godmother!"

I immediately ran to my mom, who could usually be found laying in bed or in her recliner chair if she wasn't working in the hotel or shopping. I relayed the conversation that just transpired between my aunt and I and asked if this was true. Shaking her head, she immediately asked me to get a phone book. I did as she instructed. She said, "No, his address is right there," in a very angry tone pointing to the name. When it came to something she didn't want me to find out about she would make the person, or situation, much worse than it was, and this was one of those cases. She knew that her irresponsible sibling had opened a can of worms that I would not let permanently close again.

Decades later in life, I was told that Mom had met my dad at a social in the Interlake area of Manitoba. He had a stable, good paying job as a crane operator in Manitoba. It has been said that he was the "top operator in the province of his time," according to the union. I also found out much later that my stepdad was part of the same union, Operating Engineers of Manitoba Local 987. He knew who he was, what he looked like, and had every opportunity to have him in my life if he wanted to be. I will most likely never find out the absolute truth as to why my father was not in my life, though by putting pieces together from my memories and tidbits from other people here and there, I know. The truth will lay at rest with him for now, until the research allows me to find out more truths.

I watched and learned my mom's way to navigate the waters to find out information that people were not always willing to volunteer. She was sloppy and I was a lot smarter than she had ever given me credit for. In her angry state she not only gave me the correct spelling of his name, Ted Aguesse, but now I also had his address! I was so happy with my fortune of information that I didn't know what to do. Half of me was ecstatic and the other half was scared shitless. What had happened that was so terrible that my mom would wake up during the night screaming? Oddly enough, as children, this was a regular occurrence for us. It was always a startle to be awoken this way, but didn't everyone's mom scream in the middle of the night? The plot and lies thickened. She said that part of the reason she had these bad dreams was due to the way "he" treated her. I found out later that "he" referred to a few different people, which is why I remained impartial until proven guilty. She would never be specific or give out any more information than what she thought was necessary. I assumed that she referred to my dad as "he", though I couldn't be sure. After many months of cautiously prodding, it came out that mom was quite a rebel in her time and got in some tough situations. Let's just say there were more than a few occasions, more than a few people who will remain unknown, and so many lies that to this day my mom cannot remember what the truth is. Funny thing about lies is that they accumulate. You tell one, then another to cover up that one, then another, and another, and so on until the person who started it all cannot even remember the true story of what really happened.

I needed to find out what really happened because my current source was unreliable. I decided that I would write him a letter to tell him who I was. I didn't even know if he knew about me. The fear of rejection was incredible. I didn't know what to think or do, but I had to find out some answers for myself. The only other tidbit of information that my mother told me was that I looked like him. Me, being the smartass that I was, now thought, "I knew it wasn't the milkman!" My two siblings both had straight, dark blond hair and we were nothing alike. Even in all the family pictures no one had curly, auburn hair like I had. I had a name and an address now, so I wanted to see for myself who this man was. I did not know what to expect; I did not know how he would act. There were so many "what ifs" running through my mind that I sat in front of that house on Olive Street in Winnipeg for forty-five minutes just staring, like an undercover agent. I had the letter in hand, but my mind was racing with scenarios that could happen. Would he open the door and welcome me with open arms, immediately recognizing himself in me, to finally meet the daughter he had missed out on? Would he see me as a stranger, and I would have to hand him the letter and pretend I was a messenger? Or would he see me and quickly slam the door in my face, not wanting anything to do with me as my mother had insinuated? I could not find the courage to knock on that door in fear of the reality that might follow. Fear won that battle. Maybe it was easier to "leave sleeping dogs lie," as my mother suggested.

Memories of that day in front of my dad's house never went away. As I started university, I decided to educate myself and get a great career in the hopes that one day I could still meet my dad and he would be proud of me. For many months I tried to push down the memory of that day and considered going back. I would have dreams about what our first meeting would be like. I never shared these feelings of loss and abandonment with my mother because she had made the whole situation seem so painful for her. I acknowledge that the relationship may have been traumatic for everyone involved, though there were too many pieces missing, and some stories did not line up. I understand how she could not relate to what I was feeling because she had grown up with her biological father. She had no idea and did not try to be empathetic to what I was going through. My feelings were never a concern when it came to finding out who I really was. The difficult part was that regardless of what I was ever going through, I would always find compassion in my heart to console those around me.

My university days brought a whole set of new challenges that I was excited about; independence and hopes to figure myself out the way I needed to, out from under my parents' thumb. I always knew what I needed to keep moving forward and deal with whatever came my way. I considered myself a small-town girl now moving to the city. I had no problem finding roommates and am very fortunate to have had two stable, reliable ones. Thinking about how they put up with me at times still makes me shake my head. They are some of the most patient people I know. I wanted to let myself loose on the world within reason. I was still a "good Catholic girl." I didn't drink very much, or really date. I was very shy and had low self-esteem. I showed confidence on the outside though on the inside I was a barrel of nerves. I was a full-time student and worked full-time to pay my bills. The last thing I ever wanted was to live under my parents' roof again.

One thing I need to mention about the relationship with my stepdad is that I was never scared to challenge him, while the other two children just quietly accepted whatever new boundary they, he, and my mother would try to set in place. My eldest sister would rebel by doing things behind their back, while I loved poking the bear. They tried to give me a curfew at eighteen years old at twelve o'clock. Living in the country meant driving took time to get anywhere. I went to school in Morris, Manitoba, which is twenty minutes away from Ste. Agathe, and another fifteen minutes to St. Jean Baptiste, this was where all the best socials were. Being the responsible person my parents raised, I would often be the DD (designated driver, which translated to stop drinking at eleven so I could drive myself and others home safely). Last call was at 12:30AM, and by the time the hall let out it was 1:00AM. What reasonable person would leave when the fun was just starting? Being hotel owners, they were very well aware of last calls and people who may need to get home. I made it very clear to my parents that I would leave after the last call which did not go over well, but I had my own vehicle that I paid for because I worked in the hotel as an employee since I was fifteen. This was a regular Saturday night occurrence. Just as I had to live with their guidelines, I stated mine clearly. The anger of so many lies boiled inside of me.

Throughout my life, my intuition was my guide. When I got myself in challenging situations, it was my self-doubt, guilt, and judgement that tried to ensure my purpose on Earth would not be fulfilled, but then my strength and determination usually overruled. After highschool, my parents never seemed to worry about where I was because in Ste. Agathe there was a group of five or six of my older male cousins and their friends. By including me into their circle I naturally felt the protection that I lacked growing up. We watched each other's backs when we needed to and allowed each other to make mistakes. We knew we could rely on each other to be our authentic selves in any situation. There was maternal family in this area, and I enjoyed this because I got to meet and know more of my family that I never knew I was related to. At the back of my mind, my paternal side lingered.

As I became more independent, I slowly broke away from my religious upbringing. Philosophy class encouraged me to ponder several questions about why I was even on Earth. If God was real, then why would he be continually putting me in these crazy situations that I had little to no control over? It was the first and last "all nighter" for my final in philosophy that opened more than just books. A friend and I decided that staying up all night, the day before the exam to study, was perfect to make up for our lack of commitment to the course and consistent procrastination. Red flags were everywhere. I took a nap that afternoon because there was no way I would be able to stay up all night. Being my first year in university, there was much to learn. Everyone did it so I wanted the experience. Part way through the night my friend started to cry out of nowhere describing the trauma that had suddenly been triggered. Her father had sexually abused her. WOW! I didn't see that coming! Full slap in the face for me because I never wanted to think about that crappy time in my life again. As she related her trauma, the memories of what happened with my grandfather surfaced from the vault. Rather than philosophy, we needed to talk about the trauma that was now at the surface. We guided each other while both of us adjusted to the shock. We got no sleep and had to go write an exam that would have gone better if we hadn't shown up. I am sure we looked like we had been partying all night. This was furthest from the reality of the situation. Personally, I fell asleep during the exam. I told the professor what happened and if I could please take a make-up exam. He laughed at my story and said "no." He was the first person who did not believe me. That course brought my GPA down so much that I spent an extra year in university. The floodgates were open again.

In my mind, the first and second years of university (1990-1992) were write-offs. I felt so messed up, I wasn't sure what to think. Along with other life lessons, university taught me real commitment. I kept going to school full-time at that point because my determination said, "it will take more than this to keep me down." I was also working full-time as a server and helping at the hotel when my stepdad would go away to work. He taught me how to do the day end, month end, and basic business operations while he was away because my mom felt that she was not capable of managing the hotel. Personally, I agreed and was happy that I could help, and I enjoyed the responsibility. It kept my mind off the real issue at hand: the abuse from my grandfather. I decided I needed to tell my parents what happened because I needed emotional support at this time more than ever. A small spark of faith said that they would be there for me. I told my parents that I needed to talk to them about something important. I had never been so serious in my life. My stepdad could probably see how nervous I was. When I told them that my grandfather had inappropriately touched me for about five years while we lived in Whitemouth, he came and sat beside me on the couch. My mom didn't move; she didn't believe me. I was crying and in shock. My stepdad defended me saying, "Why would she lie about something like this?" He was beside himself. He told me that when he adopted my sister and I he vowed to protect us like his own children. He had failed and there were no excuses made. This evening changed our family forever. It made sense to my stepdad though because he noticed that I would avoid my grandfather at every opportunity during family gatherings and not be around when they visited, when as a child I loved visiting my grandparents. My mom said that my mind was "playing tricks on me again." Unbelievable! I had grown close to my other aunt as well and when I told her, she didn't believe me either. This confirmed that I could not rely on my maternal family for any kind of support when I truly needed it.

Suicidal ideologies were very real at this point. In my mind, I would drive off the road at the high point and go right into the hydro pole. I could tell you the exact spot and how I was going to do it. Philosophy and university had taught me to rationalize, and I fought those inner demons viciously and it sincerely took all my strength on many occasions to talk myself out of the debilitating emotions that the saboteurs in my mind were planning. The war that was going on inside me was so raw and my heart was empty and dark. It was like a hole that could never be filled. A hole that should have been filled with compassion, empathy, support, and love. When I needed it the most, my mother's family could not set their issues aside for once and pay attention to the demons that had taken over my heart and soul. This is how I learned that I was a strong child. I was told not to show weakness, that I was the one who could survive anything. I was invincible. Saying that I felt chaos going on inside is an understatement. I contemplated different ways that I could leave the planet for good. I did not like pain and if I was going to commit suicide, I had to be certain that it would work. After all, if I survived and ended up paralyzed, like my father, or something else more challenging, there was always someone worse off, as my mother had pounded into my head. I felt that I was not meant to be born in the first place. I was unplanned, my dad didn't want me from what I knew, and my mom's family would not even try to help emotionally when I needed it. I was a zombie on the inside, full of grief and anger that no one was aware of. I kept this hidden safely. I would always think, "What if, a miracle happened, and my dad's family came looking for me and I was a wreck?" This would be even more of a reason to reject me. After all I had not been in their lives for long, why complicate anything? Though this hope that they might one day come looking for me was enough for me to pull up my socks, sort out my crap, and mentally disrupt the chaos inside.

What also kept me going was that my parents relied on me. This was my reality. Before I started working at the hotel and my stepdad went to work on the pipeline, the hotel was barely staying afloat. The extra money is what kept the doors open to the business he was so proud of. No one else in his family had owned a business (from my knowledge), and the social aspect made him feel important to the community. I brought new energy and ideas to the hotel and the bartending skills came in handy later in life when I nearly lost my house. By learning how restaurants and hotels in the city worked, I was able to implement these methods which helped the hotel become more efficient and increased revenue. When my stepdad decided to bring in computers he struggled. He brought in someone to show him the computer basics and what he needed to do to keep track of the accounting, inventory, etc. on a regular basis. He asked me to attend the orientation with the person from the computer company. Him admitting that technology was tough for him was a big deal. He said that my "brain works a lot quicker than his," so I was able to help guide him through this new transition. This was the first time he had ever truly paid me a compliment. I will not forget it because compliments were few and far between and it meant a lot. That may have been what made my life worth living. I finally had some sort of masculine support to make up for not having the biological connection. This small sign of respect from someone who had taken on the role of my dad, when mine didn't, and saw what I was capable of when it seemed no one in the family did, meant the world to me. He was reaching out to me when he needed me and I wouldn't let him down. I was the one daughter my parents always relied on.

I decided that I needed to get proper help and direction to heal from my childhood trauma, so I went to counseling. I wasn't sure what to expect from a counsellor, though my instincts told me it was the right thing to do. I was apprehensive and cautious. Opening the door to heal from the sexual abuse was easier to open than I thought. At least my stepdad believed me - I was craving emotional support. I remember being nervous about talking about all the things that I was never encouraged to talk about before. My counsellor was a young lady, maybe in her mid thirties. She had a small room where there were only two chairs, a small table which was home to a box of Kleenex, and a plant. The biggest thing was that I felt safe. When I first saw the Kleenex, I thought "okay, this may come in handy," though to be quite honest, I wasn't quite sure how I would react. My walls were high and strong, but I mentally prepared myself to talk about my grandfather since this was why I made the appointment. I needed to get rid of the anger that built up inside me. I committed to doing whatever she suggested if it helped me get to what I thought was a more stable state.

I really had trouble opening up because even though I remembered parts of what happened, there were huge gaps that I could not remember. During the third session she asked me to close my eyes to help me focus, and we did a meditation. This was my first introduction to my inner child. Of course, I knew that I had been a kid at one point, but everything I remembered was not too great. There were a lot of "sit down," "stop moving," "think before you talk," belittling, and making fun of people who I admired like Boy George of Culture Club. He was a huge influence on me because he was authentically himself. He would not let others distract him from what he believed, and he was vocal about being gay, dressing in drag, and promoting self-worth. Everything I was not and aspired to be, other than the fact that I was heterosexual.

I have always had a lot of energy. I asked a lot of questions and my mom tried to restrict this as much as she could. When I connected with my inner child for the first time, I could see this little girl who was me as a child, sitting in a corner crying. She was sad, about six or seven years old, and felt very alone because no one understood her. No one believed anything she had been through or even tried to understand who she was. It seemed as if they didn't care. In a child's mind, it is hard to comprehend the magnitude of life and all it involves. Adults kept telling this little girl to stop being who she was, be good, and do as she was told. After several weeks of counseling and a lot of inner work, I felt like I was a new person! My counsellor taught me the importance of journaling and I made it a daily habit that I still do today. She helped me answer a lot of questions but now I was mad. I was never going to let anyone hurt this little girl inside of me again! I used journaling as a tool to get rid of the anger. I would write sometimes for hours and let the emotions flow. I was brutally honest with myself and my inner child. There would be tears of joy and anger, uncertainty, and usually by the end clarity and some peace. I dove into finishing my degree and worked hard to try and make something of myself. I was determined to succeed, and nothing was going to stand in my way.

Despite my first year of study at the University of Manitoba being what I would call a year full of complications, awareness, and life lessons, I proudly graduated with an Advanced Bachelor of Arts with my focus being Social History and Women's Studies. I spent the majority of my university time making up for that year, raising my GPA. The final grade was a 2.8 which worked out to about a C+ and a pass. I gladly accepted this! It wasn't the B that I strived for, though considering I was pregnant throughout almost the entirety of my final year and still working, I am very proud of this accomplishment. My degree proved to be useful when being admitted into the Dental Assisting course and, many times throughout my career, I learned to relate to many different social classes, cultures, and people in general. Since I knew first-hand how it felt to be uncomfortable in my own skin, I ensured everyone around me was comfortable. This sacrifice of self was a lesson I learned from my mom.

CHAPTER 8

After a Life of Being Cautious, I Threw Caution to the Wind

During the last year of university my world got turned upside down. I had not had very much luck dating because the armour I held was very strong and I liked it that way. An old friend from Whitemouth and I ran into each other at the mall. Since it was my birthday, we agreed to go out that weekend to catch up at a local club. To my surprise she had invited a fellow co-worker, Jon. I never thought anything of it because it was my birthday, and we were in a public place. I was polite and we spoke for a bit, but I was not attracted to him. Without my permission she gave him my phone number. When she told me I was angry because it was so disrespectful, and I would not have given him my number. I did not need the hassle. Between work and school, a random guy was the last thing I needed in my life. When I spoke with him, I could feel red flags everywhere. My intuition had grown since I had just finished counseling and was developing a strong relationship with my inner child. I had just gotten back on my emotional feet, getting ready to establish a good career. He became an unwelcome distraction. He had a weird hairstyle, was very arrogant, and was not my type. He phoned one, two, three times and would not take "No" for an answer, so I threw caution to the wind. I thought, "It's a coffee date, what is the worst thing that could happen?"

Dating at 22 years old was still foreign for me. I was not encouraged to date even though I had many male friends. I was known as the "good girl" in town because any kind of physical activity, even hand holding, was uncomfortable for me. Thinking back, I can remember boys trying to sit closer to me or saying things that were supposed to signify that they were interested in some sort of relationship. A large part of my apprehension was due to having a low self-esteem from my childhood trauma which included no biological father. Looking at me you would never guess because I did what I wanted and dressed how I thought was appropriate. I never dressed outlandish or showed too much skin - my religious upbringing took care of that. Every time someone had shown obvious interest, I would say "No" and ensure they never bothered me again with very rude comments. The group of guys I hung out with were cousins or their friends, and I became part of their group. It never amounted to more than that because I had very firm boundaries. My parents never worried because as a group, we respected each other. My parents saw this when we would interact, which was every weekend at the local bar and during the week at my parents' establishment. My parents probably felt good about this because they could supervise. This was a happy time in my life. The people I hung out with accepted me for who I was, and it was never questioned, nor did they try to steer me away from what was important to me and my career.

Jon and I dated for two or three weeks simply because he was so persistent. In the back of my mind, I was wondering "What is wrong with this guy that he is so interested in me?" I never realized it at the time due to my secluded dating life, but the relationship was stalker-like. He had to know where I was all the time, when he could see me, what I was doing, and it got to the point where I said this is too much and broke up with him. Ste. Agathe, where I worked at my parents' hotel, is located 20-minute drive to the perimeter of the city. He lived in the city center, did not have a vehicle, had a minimum wage job, and barely graduated high school. Not the kind of person I saw myself sharing my life with. I realize that some people are more hands-on for work like construction. At least that could be a career with benefits, decent salary, pension, and allowed you to reach higher levels depending on which trade you are in. He was not even that. He easily found fault with everyone around him, including my group of friends, and had excuses as to why they were at fault. He did not take the breakup well. He rode his bike out to come talk to me. When he pulled up and I saw him I felt like I hit a brick wall. I thought I was clear: NO means NO, but apparently not to him. Since I was working, and he just cycled for probably 3 hours, I agreed to give him another chance. I will admit that I was flattered that he made such an effort to come see me. I told my instincts to relax because I looked at all his effort. He must really love me! If I could give myself advice then from who I am now, I would tell her to call the cops. Listen to those sirens going off inside. They are doing that for a reason! Even my friends thought that I was crazy. They were shocked that I would even entertain the idea of seeing him again. I was so headstrong that when I made up my mind, I made up my mind. This was between Jon and I, and he loved me. Relationships have ups and downs, and these are normal when someone loves you. I convinced myself that everything was going to be okay; I lied to myself. My longing for true, unconditional love was so great that I sacrificed the love for my inner child.

We had only known each other for three months when I got pregnant. I was taking the pill, but we were those people who are the one percent that it may not work for. Of course, he didn't like wearing a condom and I didn't know any different, so I listened and followed his lead. Being sexually active was new territory for me. After a visit to my family doctor, she had told me that I had been pregnant before this pregnancy. I was shocked and denied it, but it never left my mind. I appreciated her making me more aware. I was shy because I had never spoken about this stuff with anyone on a personal level. I remembered a few weeks prior when I had cramps and saw something weird in the toilet. It felt like something odd when I peed that morning, as if something "fell out." I remember taking a close look in the toilet, but did not put two and two together. This was all new territory. I dismissed the idea in my head that I had just lost a baby. That would mean I had been pregnant. I remember the shape of the embryo - I would have been about 2-3 months pregnant. I remember the shape of a head, premature eyes, curled spine, and tail as if it was a tadpole. This was my first child. Throughout my life the name Stephan kept popping up here and there, but I wasn't sure why so again I dismissed signs that the universe was trying to tell me. Much later in life, when my children had moved out and were in their mid-twenties, this is one of the blocks that a tantric helped me remove. The embryo was a little boy. He came to me in a dream, needing to be loved and cared for. Without hesitation I loved him instantly, just as I had done with my other children. I would not allow this child to be loved conditionally as I had been. He came to me with long, messy, unkempt hair that was full of knots, tattered clothing, and very insecure. He needed to be loved and shown guidance. I saw him standing near me unsure with his head down wondering if I would abandon him again. My heart broke as I realized who he was. I would never abandon him again. Instead, I reached out to him by the hand and guided him home. I cleaned him up, gave him new clothes, cut his hair, fed him, and cuddled with him while I read him a book. I provided him with the love that he longed for unconditionally, just as I had consciously. His name is now Stephan, and I was able to introduce him to my paternal side spiritually. My dad held out his hand and Stephan went to him easily as if reuniting with his grandfather. He was finally with family, the family that was now able to support and love him.

This is what tantric healing does. Tantric allows you to connect spiritually with loved ones that may need you for whatever reason. In Stephan's case, he was a lost soul. With guidance from my shaman, I was able to bring peace to this part of my life. There were so many feelings that were missing that contributed to my feelings of not being whole. When the miscarriage happened, I had pushed down wanting to feel any of the emotions that would come with losing a child. My life had been hard and was often turned upside down. The universe knew I would not be able to handle more. In my family, there was the thought that God will only give you what you can handle, and this is evidence. I most likely could not endure more in my early twenties. He came to me when I was 51 years old. I asked for the unprocessed emotions to surface so that I would become a vibrational match to guide others to the best of my abilities. I let Stephan know how unconditionally he is loved. I did not know how to love myself as a young adult; no one had shown me. Now I understand that you cannot love anyone else unconditionally unless you love yourself first. As they say, put the oxygen mask on yourself first or you will be no good to anyone. This knowledge would grow after the birth of my second child.

The brick wall that I was pregnant again became very real, and I kept pushing down the feelings and ignored the fact that this relationship was very toxic because Jon said he loved me. It took a little while for it to sink in that I would become a mother to someone who I already loved though I was scared as hell. This meant that I would be connected to Jon on a different level, and it was very uncomfortable. I was in my last year of university with my whole life ahead of me. There were a million things running through my head. I vowed that my child would never have to feel the abandonment or conditional love that I went through. Surprisingly, I was not as nervous as I thought I would be to tell my parents I was pregnant. I still had a lot of anger to work through, and this was a way to prove to them what a better parent I would be. My parents didn't talk to me for 3 months after I gave them the news. I am not sure why I thought they would be more supportive than they were. Maybe because of everything my mom went through, I felt she would understand and for once be there for me so she could make up for the mistakes she had made. WRONG! When she said, "You made your bed now lie in it," I was shocked and felt as though they threw me to the wolves. I remember how disappointed I felt that again they were not there for me. Just as they weren't before. So much for the idea that they could try to be compassionate. I stood tall - this was not my first rodeo and I thought that like I had figured most other things out on my own, I would figure this out as well. I officially decided that I didn't need them anymore, I was tired of all of it. I had a new family now that said and showed that they loved me. This was all that seemed to matter. Jon's family was surprised though supportive. They were excited for us.

My parents soon realized if they wanted to keep any sort of relationship with me and their soon-to-be grandchild, they needed to accept the situation. I made it crystal clear that I would not have an abortion, nor would I give my baby up for adoption. I was also told that adoption was not an option because Jon's family would adopt the baby, and I would then not be able to see the baby again. Jon's family appeared to be supportive though there was a lot of manipulation. I minimized many things even though again, there were red flags everywhere. They said they loved me, and they told me that when people truly love you, they are protective. They explained that what I saw as aggression and jealousy was them showing how much they loved me. I had never experienced behavior like this. I remember being eight months pregnant and Jon pushed me on the bed, knowing how unbalanced I was with the extra weight. I was shocked and completely scared for the first time in my life as he laughed at me, then took advantage of my state.

I had a lot of freedom from the age of 11 until now. Jon's family used the word love like it was second nature to them. They always greeted people with a hug and kiss and were affectionate with each other. Being European, I was told this was normal. Traditionally, other people in my extended stepdad's family had greeted each other similarly so I accepted it. It was my maternal family that was unaffectionate and could not show feelings. Jon's family could also be very aggressive. Not being raised around boys, and as Jon had two brothers, I thought the fighting was normal because this is what I was told and saw on TV. At times it seemed over the top, but I minimized it. Punching holes in the walls and breaking furniture or other material objects was not a daily occurrence, though it was something they were used to. Be aware that threats and ultimatums are NEVER a sign of love.

My son was born on May 5, 1995, at 3:48PM. Anything I had known before about love went out the window - that was conditional. I never thought it was possible to love a human so fiercely and unconditionally. I had so many emotions running through my mind. I was scared, unsure, protective, compassionate, and determined. I promised him that I would be the best mother that I could be and I meant it with all my heart and soul. Jon was somewhat helpful at first, though it was my mother-in-law who really came through for me. I will always be grateful for the lessons she taught me on how to care for a baby. I had done a lot of babysitting as a teenager but never with a newborn. She taught me how to nurse him with my body and explained how breastfeeding was not only the healthiest for the baby, but it also strengthened the bond between us. Of course, raising my son took a toll on me physically and mentally. I was determined to learn everything that I could on how to raise a baby. I wanted to make the right choices with his best interest in mind. He was my ultimate priority! I read books, listened intently to my wise, unconditionally loving mother-in-law, and truly savoured every moment with him. The book series "*What to Expect When ...*" became my Bible.

My mother-in-law took the time to teach me about cooking, caring for a family, and general life tasks that my mom never took the time to do. The big difference between the two of them was that my mother-in-law taught me from her heart because she saw early on that my mom was not a hands-on, nurturing type of person. My mother was more of a "throw her in the deep end and see if she swims," type of teacher. Even when my mom tried to show us how to do something, putting any amount of love into the task was difficult for her. I love my mom, and I will be forever grateful to her for bringing me into this world, but she did not love herself, which was a true reflection on my siblings and I. She spent most of my childhood in victim or survival mode. It was only on a special occasion like Christmas, New Year's Eve, or Easter when she would dress up because there would be a family function. The only make-up she wore was lipstick. Taking care of herself daily was not a thing, and it was always the bare minimum. What I have learned from her was how important it is to love yourself first so that you are capable of loving others.

She was unaware of the ancestral burdens that she carried with her and now passed on to us. This was unintentional because I know she did the best she could with what she knew and would have done better if those ancestral chains were not so heavy. What I mean when I reference ancestral chains is how each person has their own journey, or life path on earth, and whether it is positive or negative, this greatly impacts the outcome. To explain clearer, all your family from over a thousand years ago did what they needed to do to survive. Those people made choices, good or bad, depending on the circumstances they were in. Some were good hunters; some were better at prioritizing what needed to be done to keep living another day. This is where Darwin's "Survival of the Fittest," comes in. Those who were not able to make the necessary decisions for survival perished. Your brain, the amygdala portion or what some refer to as the reptilian brain, was the protector and responsible for fight or flight from danger. As the frontal lobe portion of your brain evolved, you became who you are today. Limiting beliefs were reinforced with each new challenge. Your ancestors had their own challenges to stay alive and in some cases be successful. Each family has their own journey.

Getting back to my family as an example, there was a lot of abuse towards each other because they just needed to make it to the next day (many families can relate). Many women were not considered people until the 1900s depending on which country or province you grew up in. Mental health only started to be talked about in the late 70s and 80s, and this was only if your family was open minded. Mine was not. An easy way to think of this in a spiritual sense could be that for every limiting belief, another link is added to the chain. In some cases, a new link was formed and in others the link or limiting belief was reinforced. The initial belief only got stronger. By the time these emotional and mental or spiritual chains are attached to the living, they are so heavy that the body rebels. This rebellion displays itself in forms of illnesses, rashes, genetically inherited diseases, and so on. At this point I want to reinforce that every one of your ancestors had a choice. Whether they made a decision that was beneficial or was detrimental to survival is a reflection of how heavy those chains are. The past is in the past and you cannot change the past. All you can do is help your ancestors rid themselves of the guilt and judgement so they can be at peace. Everyday you have a new opportunity to make choices to make your life better than it was the day before. Becoming fully aware of your environment and making the decision to make it better is all up to you!

To say that Jon came from a very toxic family is an understatement. Every type of abuse was present, though to a much higher degree than I had experienced. I can remember arriving to pick up my ex-mother-in-law, who did not drive, to go to a cultural event where she was a big deal. She was an amazing cook, and the pavilion knew that they could rely on her to provide the best representation from her and her skills of their culture. I knew my dad's family were French, though at the time I did not know that they were from Europe. Subconsciously, I gravitated towards male figures that I thought would be like my dad. I was proud of my mother-in-law and her achievements. She put love into everything she did. She was ready to go as expected, though she was not herself and I could feel something was off. My ex-sister-in-law quickly put a scarf around her neck, but not before I noticed the strangle marks. I couldn't stop staring. The look of shame and embarrassment on my mother-in-law's face was all I needed as confirmation that my suspicions were correct. She and her husband were fighting again, and he was physically, mentally, emotionally, and sexually abusive. My father-in-law was a man who grew up with a substantial amount of trauma. My mother-in-law and her children were all truly victims of the household wrath. Very deep ancestral toxicity prevailed in this family, but this was way before I was even aware that this existed.

In Jon's family, everyone was on their best behavior at first. I experienced love from my ex and his family that were totally foreign to me. For the first time in my life, I heard the words "I love you." This roller coaster of emotions when people are very nice then out of nowhere turn violent is known as emotional abuse. This is the hardest abuse to detect because the level of uncontrolled anger and manipulation that "it really isn't that bad" is real. I kept telling myself this because I was stuck in this situation with an infant, no physical, or emotional support from my own family and literally scared for my life, and that of my son's life, at times. It was a reality that I could never allow them to take my son back home "to visit" because I may never see him again. These threats were consistent throughout our relationship! I developed a much thicker skin and had to figure a way out. I would minimize the situation because everyone has bad days, and no one is perfect. The family was also strictly religious, much more than my family. When Jon started talking about getting married, I wasn't sure what to think. I could clearly see that my son and I would not spend the rest of our lives with him, but at that moment what was I to do? It was told to me very clearly that we had a child out of wedlock and would go to Hell if we didn't correct things, so we got married in the Orthodox church. I liked their traditional marriage ceremony and with us "doing the right thing" maybe it would take the pressure off us.

I got married for all the wrong reasons. On the day of my wedding there were red flags, though I didn't listen to my inner self because I didn't want to let anyone down. Everyone was excited, including me. I had high hopes that our relationship would get better and some sort of normalcy would prevail. As I finished getting ready at the back of the church and even when my stepdad walked me down the aisle, I knew I was getting married for many of the wrong reasons. We had a child without being married; my spidey senses were tingling big time and I was ignoring them because I wanted to be married, I just was not sure if it was supposed to be to him. His family was religious and were putting a lot of pressure on him to get married as well. On my side it was my grandparents putting pressure on my mom who passed this anxiety onto me. Like how our ancestral stories are passed on, this is another way generational trauma is furthered. They only wanted us to do what they thought was right for them. People treat single parents differently than parents who are married.

On our wedding night I remember feeling obligated to consummate the marriage so "let's get this over with," was my attitude. I still was not attracted to him, and I remember thinking that I needed to follow tradition since I didn't know any difference and this is what all the books, movies, and society said was "right." I kept telling myself lies like, "no one is perfect", "maybe I will grow to love him as I am supposed to...whatever that looks like," and "there is always someone worse off than me." I had envisioned a fairy-tale wedding. I didn't know what a good marriage looked like because I had so many traumatic ones around me. There was a lot of yelling, women being "put in their place," intimidating actions like slamming fists on counters, slamming doors, kitchen chairs getting thrown around, name calling, belittling, jealousy, and swearing were all regular behaviour from Jon. What I saw historically was that when a woman would stick up for herself it was seen as disrespectful. My mom had said, "You never know what goes on behind closed doors," and that was us. On the honeymoon we went to a small resort just for the weekend. We were leaning on the railing overlooking the pool the day after the marriage discussing last names. Jon gave me the ultimatum that if I did not take his last name, he would leave me, and I would never see my son again. He would not take no for an answer and did not want to discuss the option of hyphenating our names. This is when I knew I was in marriage jail. I was beside myself. I changed my last name, going against every fiber of my being. Through this, I lost even more of my identity. I tried to accept that this is the way my life would be because as my mother said, "I made my bed, now I have to lay in it." I had to be responsible for my situation. I was now married to someone that I had to make the best of the situation with, and I had to make choices differently to protect my baby. I knew I had to be strong, and I also knew that I had to adapt to this new part of my journey because my most cherished possession, my son, depended on me.

CHAPTER 9

"I Do... ???"

Marriage today has many definitions. Some people enter this union for reasons not of love but of financial security, fantasy from watching too many old Disney movies, or because they feel it is the right thing to do at the time. The sanctity of marriage, as I was raised, is between a man and a woman who respect, cherish, and support each other equally as one, presenting a unified front. This has changed over my lifetime as my new definition of marriage represents two people not necessarily the same gender, who love and support each other as one. This has been a very difficult concept for me since my first marriage was forced by others more religious than myself and my ex-husband. The second marriage was partly an escape from the realities that my life presented to me, though I did enter this marriage full of love and respect for him and his family. I thought this was mutual, though the same evidence comes up again where you need to heal and love yourself first before you can love another person. This was the case with my second ex-husband.

My first marriage represents the first time that I felt I had a family that loved me unconditionally. They accepted me for the most part, but not members of my family. They saw how my family did not display affection and how raising my son was seen as an obligation, not an act of love. Love as I defined it was the deep affection that I felt for my son that could not be explained. There was always a curtain to protect us from the world as I saw it. I felt as if I was on my own in protecting him and was forced to accept certain aid due to my life situation. Sounds familiar, yes; I consistently compared my life to that of my mother's and vowed not to repeat it, though some things were out of my control. I was able to experience the struggles that my mother may have had firsthand now. At twenty-four years old I finally understood the sacrifice she had made by keeping me rather than putting me up for adoption.

The manipulation and abuse was raw and real. This first attempt to allow someone into my heart after my grandfather reinforced the concept that I was not worthy of real love. Men were an enemy because I should not have to fight so hard just to be heard and respected. I got more than crushed; I was raped and experienced mental/sexual/emotional abuse, but thankfully was able to get divorced. I had three children with Jon. My grandfather had passed away the year before and my second son was 3 months old. Jon had become a different person and I was half-convinced that things were getting better for our young family. Yes, there were many occurrences that I consistently made excuses for, but I wanted our relationship to work out with all my heart. It wasn't perfect but it was a work in progress, just as any relationship. Jon found issues with any counselors we tried, and we tried many. It was always a problem with them, not him. He took no responsibility for how our relationship was a constant struggle. The truth is that he was not raised with emotionally healthy role models either, so this made life even harder for us.

NO MEANS NO! Without getting graphic, I was so empty inside and I knew I didn't love him. I hated not only the way he treated me but also the way I allowed him to get away with it. The daily walking on eggshells was only the tip of the iceberg. The swearing, name calling, and forcing himself on me were a daily part of my life. I would tell him that I didn't love him and how much I hated the way he treated me, but this fell on deaf ears. This sexual abuse was something that I have had to work through decades psychologically to heal. To try and avoid him, I would go to bed fully clothed, try to keep my legs closed (which he would pry open), amongst other things. He was physically stronger than me. I am talking about this so other women, and men, can relieve themselves of the guilt and confusion surrounding their body's reaction to forced intercourse - rape. This includes things like orgasm as an involuntary reaction in an abusive situation. By understanding how the body works, the empowerment is great and will help you to make different choices, thereby aiding you to get out of the situation. In a nutshell, the stages as defined by www.herstory.global discuss how psychologically the body's reaction, thanks to our reptilian brain or amygdala, is the most basic and goes into survival mode. I was not able to use my "fight or flight" instincts because he was stronger than me, so I went into a temporary paralysis mode to survive. An article by Vice from June 6, 2017, describes perfectly how it felt to be raped regularly. I would mentally tell myself, *just get it over with so he will leave.* He was persistent and no was not an option, (like my grandfather) he would follow me around the house. If I knew he was home and we would be by ourselves, I learned to stay away until I could go get the kids. My loss of control was frightening and overwhelming, though I felt by abandoning my sense of self and my security, I was protecting my young family. I wanted to avoid a much worse situation that I had witnessed in his parents' home. Throwing toys at my son rather than playing with him broke my heart. He did not deserve this either. I was frozen and I did not know how to safely leave this situation. When the other two children arrived, his pattern became more predictable, so I was able to protect myself and them differently. Slowly, I felt I was getting strong enough to take a bold action to get him out of our home.

The PTSD (Post Traumatic Stress Disorder) affected me for decades. The depression, guilt, overwhelming feelings, anxiety, confusion, and lack of identity contributed to the person I no longer recognised. No one knew what went on behind closed doors. They thought we were a family with a couple of struggles just like many young couples when learning to manoeuvre through this phase of their life journey. I became someone I no longer recognised. When he left the home I shared with my children, I got a protection order for our safety. He tried to tell me I was blowing things out of proportion and being unreasonable. Was I really? I knew what I felt, and I still had enough of myself left to know that not only was this behavior toxic and abusive, but only I could make the changes necessary for my children to live happy, healthy lives. Relationships were not easy for me. If I met someone nice, I would easily find something wrong because I was not accustomed to someone treating me the way I deserved, like finding a good office to work in. I would become someone I wasn't to test how far people would go in treating me poorly. This originates from not knowing my biological father. The abandonment and feelings of not being good enough ran deep, just as many of my ancestors had experienced. This had to stop!

When my daughter was born, she brought with her the extra strength that I needed to pick myself up and kick him out of our home. The name calling, belittling, intimidation, fear, controlling, alienation, and rape were a regular occurrence for us now. Ten days after I had given birth to my daughter, he forced himself on me, tearing the 13 stitches that were from the episiotomy and it got infected. When the nurse came by to check up on me, I will never forget the look on her face as she looked up from inspecting whatever was causing the soreness down there. Ethically and morally, she should have made a report to someone, even my general practitioner. She knew what had happened, the evidence was right in front of her. I was in an abusive situation that I did not know how to get out of. At my visit to the GP, the nurse explained what she saw so the GP was aware as well. I was so ashamed that I made excuses or said nothing. My face said everything. I literally felt like there was a black hole where my heart used to be. My self-esteem was at an all time low, but I had felt this before when I had contemplated suicide. My motivation was now the three little people that I had sworn to protect by bringing them into this world. I would look at them and force myself to activate a plan to kick him out. I was not the person being abusive, I would not leave. The last thing I wanted was for my children to grow up in this chaotic, traumatic situation thinking that it was normal. I spoke with a lawyer, developed a game plan, and on February 15, 2000, he was removed from the property. We would be much safer. I had a protection order placed against him for the safety of myself and my children. This was much more than distrust for him, I feared what he may do because he had gotten unpredictable.

I will define from my experience what a psychological or emotionally abusive relationship is. In an emotionally abusive relationship, the predator (Jon) will prey on the victims' (myself and my children) emotions and target weaknesses so that the victim becomes totally under their control. Jon was very jealous of my education. He would make fun of it, and not be supportive of continuing to develop my career. He ensured this would not happen by raping me to exert his control over me. He now expected me to stay at home, pop out children, and raise them with the façade that we were a happy little family. The predator makes you think and believe that you cannot survive without them. They are possessive and insecure in themselves so they do not trust anyone and will blame you for anything. They twist your words, which develops what some people term "crazymaking". They will alienate you from any supportive friends or family. The constant walking on eggshells raises the daily anxiety through the roof.

A couple years after we separated, he told me that he had been diagnosed as bipolar. My first thought was, "Well that makes a lot of sense but kind of late." He tried now to make our relationship work for the children's sake, but this was all superficial. While going through the divorce, he had two lawyers dismiss him because they witnessed his irresponsible behavior continuously. I had witnessed the monster he could become. Rather than allowing the victimized little boy to prevail into the man he was meant to be, the monster was his choice. The young boy who was punished in grade school for using his left hand was who I fell in love with… did he deserve this? Of course not. That was fifty years ago. The potential of who he and I could become is what kept me hopeful. He was too weak to see this, and I now had three children to care for. I did not need a fourth. He had many opportunities to rectify his wrongs. When making a choice he always made himself the priority, not us. I knew life would be hard as a single parent, though much easier on my own than with him.

I consistently had to remind myself that breaking up the family was the right decision for us at the time. If I would not have made this decision, I feel strongly that my children would have suffered even more from the abuse than what they did. I ensured that the children and I would remain in the duplex that had a fenced-in yard, were close to many community supports, and that it was stable for us. Jon was the one who provided the loss as an absent father and even male role model. Perhaps one day he will realize how he could have done things differently instead of always blaming others.

For years my children blamed me for breaking up our family because I kept my secrets hidden until now. Full disclosure, I am aware that each of them will interpret this part of my life differently because they are different people. I love my children more than they may ever realize though I know with an open mind, an open heart, and this new information, they will understand why I made some of the choices I did and have forgiven myself for making them as I heal. By breaking the cycle for them and future generations, my story provides the strength to make different choices for different actions. Words meant nothing to my ex-husband, though he spoke a lot and expected everyone else to listen. I have learned to ignore some people's words because they are just talking without providing meaning; I believe that actions speak much louder than words. I have learned to efficiently distinguish between those who are trying to pull the wool over my eyes and those people who genuinely mean what they say.

It took a long time, and I wondered if I would ever be able to forgive Jon, but I did. I have done the work, worked through the tremendous amount of anger and pain, to get to where I am now. I can be at peace knowing that inside he will be the person I fell in love with. After a recent phone call where I intended to send him love and forgiveness over the phone, within thirty seconds I had to end our conversation for my own protection. He made me learn about forgiveness, love, and gratitude, so I thank you Jon for providing the traumatic lessons that you did. They made me so much stronger and helped me to reach levels that I never thought possible. I never realized that a person could carry as much anger and hate as I had. I sincerely hope that one day you can try to rediscover the inner child that you forgot about from so long ago. He needs you desperately and requires some guidance. The best part of the relationship was that I birthed three amazing children which I am very proud of. It took a few decades to truly appreciate the many lessons, forgive, and learn how to love again.

I knew on a surface level that I needed to heal from the trauma that the marriage and divorce brought to me. It was recommended that group counselling would be the most beneficial and I agreed. For the first time I didn't feel alone, there were other women out there who had been through similar traumas and had different coping strategies that I could adopt and use what worked best. I still use many of these strategies today to stay grounded. I went from surviving to becoming the best mother I could be so my children would be proud to call me their mom. Even moreso, I would be proud of myself to the core. I did my best to protect them and now was able to make proper decisions for their benefit, like ensuring supervised visitation and that the daycare would only allow me or someone I gave permission to to pick them up.

When I picked myself up and went back to school, I changed my whole routine and became the resourceful person that I am today. Since

I am Metis, I ensured that all my children had their ID card in case we needed help. The Manitoba Metis Federation paid for my Level II Dental Assistant course including Orthodontic and Scaling modules and living expenses. I could never have established this career without their guidance. I journaled at night and exercised in the morning to get rid of the constant anxiety and pressures to do well. I drove myself so hard that I fell into survival mode without realizing what I had done. Most of this pressure was put on me by myself because I chose to be a single parent, and I would not fail to still be a better parent than how my parents were. I had friends and an amazing day care full of people who genuinely cared for my children. They were my new guide to help me parent. They went above and beyond for me, and I showed my appreciation with small gifts like baking or shared babysitting, especially later with the rigorous hockey schedule. They say it takes a community to raise a child and this is so true! I told myself that I am the role model that I needed as a child. By going back to school and working very hard with my children to ensure they were happy, fed, clothed, and growing in an environment they needed to be, I ensured they were emotionally healthy.

I can remember times after I rid myself of my toxic relationship and concentrated on resurrecting the lives that my children deserved and needed. I fell into survival mode because I was so focused on not failing for my children. The current job I had as a caregiver to clients who had mental and physical disabilities did not pay well and I was not receiving child support. I was going through the motions day by day until one day I was helping my aunt pack some boxes and saw the photo of my daughter crawling. It hit me like a brick wall because I didn't recognise her. My aunt told me who it was, and I started crying. I had to get out of my head and raise them from my heart. I still had a lot of anger that needed to be processed and gotten rid of. Any of the furniture that Jon and I had acquired was sold, donated, or disposed of. This was the first time in my life that I could understand what the term "cleaning house" meant. Boy did I clean the house! I understood that by making the decision to become a single parent, I would need to do many things that I had never done before with confidence, so that my children did not know how scared I truly was of messing up their lives. I put fear aside and strength became my new superpower.

With furniture and material items gone, the open spaces provided the perspective that I required to start fresh with my children, who were six, three, and two years old now. I tore out carpet that was throughout the house in the living room, kitchen (yes, kitchen), and stairs to find beautiful, original hardwood floors. In the basement the bottom half of the walls were covered with panelling that looks like wood from the 70s. This was all removed. I learned the amazing use of paint, how to remove wallpaper, and learned to fill in and repair holes, provided by my ex. Thank you for these lessons, Jon. I became quite a good renovator as I researched, refurbished, and made our environment new and so much more ours. The kids rooms had themes which I never had; Toy Story for the boys with homemade curtains. I put up shelves and sewed a stuffed T-rex for the corner of the room. My daughter had royal purple on the bottom half and princess pink on the top half with a border in the middle that had pretty butterflies, bugs, and flowers. Her dresser handles were bug and flower shapes. These were rooms I was proud to provide to them and did so on an extremely tight budget. I did a lot of sewing to calm my nerves because each item was made with love, whether it was curtains for the kids' rooms, pjs for Christmas, or their own unique Christmas stockings, and two years in a row I was able to provide the costumes for my daughter's dance class. I never realized it until years later when my eldest said that he would often fall asleep to the humming of the sewing machine. He knew that there was a new creation evolving, usually for them. I was doing something right as I replaced the stress and anger for love.

No longer did I have the toxicity of Jon's memories around me daily. Thanks to lessons from my grandfather and stepfather, I learned to drywall, paint, place vinyl flooring, and became confident fixing whatever was needed around the house. As the kids grew, they referred to me as the "Mom-Dad" because it was only me providing both roles for them. My uncle's career was at CN Rail as the supervisor for electrical signals on the lines across Canada. He taught me how to change electrical outlets, light switches, and overhead lights. The things I paid someone to do for me were refinishing the floors and relining the bathtub lining. I knew that the floors would be impossible with three little ones running around and I knew nothing about plumbing. Our house was now our home. I took great pride in the house and the yard that I was able to provide for my children. My parents provided material items for the grandchildren like a swing set, sandbox, and pool that had a dolphin in the middle that sprayed water out of its blowhole. Emotionally, I healed myself with the tools learned from the counselling that I continued like nightly journaling.

Growing up and being strong required sacrifice. I had learned and accepted that my feelings and that whatever happened to me were secondary to raising my children. This was a decision that I made to protect their emotional, physical, and mental wellbeing. This reminder was consistent. My children were the daily reminder that I needed to keep doing better and that I was going to get us through this. I was determined to learn what I needed to provide normalcy to my children's lives. Jon's contribution to child support was unreliable and extremely sporadic. When I would find out where he was working, which changed often because he would consistently get laid off or fired, I had to report this to Maintenance Enforcement so that child support could get deducted from his wages. The amount that we did get usually caught us up on bills and I ensured the kids and I did something fun. This went on for the remainder of the children's childhood until they turned eighteen. Growing up without my biological father I knew how important it was to have him in their lives to some capacity. I would provide sports schedules, plan for them to have supervised visits, and encourage phone calls. Jon made the decisions he made to not be in his children's life, but at least I provided the opportunity. I learned to accept his irresponsible behavior as he would rarely attend a hockey game or swim lesson and never attended an achievement. The most difficult part was handling the disappointed children every time he failed to follow through on basic fatherly duties. To protect my children's emotional well being, I stopped providing the opportunities for disappointment. It became evident that any kind of interaction would be on his terms. His selfish behavior resonated loudly. The children loved the idea of having a father within reach physically, though emotionally he would not respond to their cries for attention. I could no longer entertain him and his circus of emotional and mental abuse.

Relationships were difficult as part of me was looking for that father figure that the children needed. In the end, my stepdad proved to be a good grandfather to them as he taught them many outdoor hobbies and became the male role model they lacked for guy stuff. My parents had a seasonal camping spot so we would pitch our tent every weekend in their lot and camp with them. We had a bit of privacy; it got us out of the city and in a worse case scenario they were there to help if I needed it. Repairing the relationship with my parents was difficult, but I believe we needed each other. I showed my parents, specifically my mother, how to show love, and my stepdad got grandchildren that he could show off his fishing skills to. My children were showered with affection daily! They would grow up knowing how much I loved them, and my stepdad ensured they knew how much I sacrificed to give them everything I could.

Dating was hit and miss, and I started to worry about being alone. The children were between the ages of 8-12 years old and were going to start developing lives of their own. I realized that I could not depend on them as my source of comfort and motivation. I decided to get remarried.

Deep in my soul, I do still believe in the sanctity of marriage. I had tried dating companies and online sites which I thought taught me the basics of how to sift through the bs and find a quality person. I met my second husband on April Fool's Day - that was a sign right there! He was a good person deep down, but like most of us he already had a failed marriage. I ignored all the red flags because something told me that for whatever reason I needed to get closer to my paternal family. I did not realize it when I was getting to know him, but my father's family lived an hour away from where we lived, which was five minutes north of Warren, Manitoba. I fell in love with his silliness; he was a hard worker and, as he put it, "was able to MacGyver almost anything." The parts that I ignored were the finances, warning signs even from his mother regarding how irresponsible he was. How well did I really know him before we got married in 2008? In hindsight the marriage should have been annulled, though I gave him the benefit of the doubt and I trusted that he had good intentions. He brought two more children to the brood which conveniently provided us with five children all a year apart, so it was easy to remember the ages and birthdays.

This marriage held many lessons, challenges, and insights which gravitated more and more towards my paternal family. The Universe provides in odd ways, and it was not until over a decade after we divorced that the signs fell into place and I started to understand the cosmic energy that was guiding me. We dated for a year and a half before we got married, though I lived in the city and he was in the country. He was able to survive by himself because his mother enabled him by providing him with the tools to keep getting into situations that he was not learning from. He was a good person and loved to help friends or family when needed. His extended family was educated, hardworking, and aware of the situation I was getting into. They had learned to keep to themselves because they had been burnt trying to help as well. He was still stuck in his old marriage. Legal terminology that I had sheltered my children from was now out in the open because his children were aware of the terms, but were stuck in the situation they were in. At first, I thought that I could help smooth the situations over with the children and his ex, but he had so much anger and immaturely fought with his ex consistently to the point that his children became victims of the games they played against each other. I realized very quickly that again, I needed to get my children out of this situation. I could see how our marriage would only get worse. I married someone who I thought was a good role model, though his demons were stronger than him. He told so many lies that he couldn't keep them straight, alcohol was his best friend, and he was very irresponsible with his finances.

While he was living in the rural area for the first year of our marriage, my children and I were living in the city preparing to sell our house and tie up loose ends with school and sports. At the time the only thing that I kept thinking was that I was getting back to living in the country, which provided the peace and room I needed to calm my mind, and it was time for a new beginning. I had worked hard to get myself back to a stable place mentally and emotionally. The country living also provided a calm area and room for my children as we outgrew our home. The chaos that we were welcomed to hit me like a brick wall. I had ignored the many red flags rather than listening to my intuition. I was ashamed and embarrassed that I allowed myself and my children to be put in this situation; although, I again held my head high and tried not to listen to all the judgement around me. I needed to rescue myself again. I surrendered to whoever was listening at that point: God, the universe, angels. I had to pick myself up again for the sanity of my children who were in dire need to be on our own again. I rented a storage unit and filled it with our belongings. He did not even notice. I let the children in on the plan, and right under his nose, we packed and moved many of the items. On the day of the move, there was only furniture left to move. When I told him that we were leaving it felt like a relief to us both. We had merely been roommates for the last two years living together. He was depressed and not able to get out of it, his only concern was the property. I surrendered this to be able to move on in an efficient fashion. I found a house minutes further north, towards my unknown family. Interestingly, the children went to school in St. Laurent, Mb., which was only thirty minutes from my dad's town, Deerhorn. We were getting closer and closer to my paternity, and I was not even aware. This universal pull towards my paternal family was strong. All I knew was that it felt right. It took me four years to get us out of that marriage.

I relied on my resourceful nature once again as my navigational skills were activated. The marriage was simple, so I was able to do the divorce myself with guidance from law students. This was a learning curve, but I had always been interested in law, so I was eager to learn and understand the process. The kids were able to stay in the schools they were in, and we established our home in Woodlands.

As the children grew into teenagers, I moved on for myself and realized that they would have to make hard decisions one day as well. I took solace in the fact that I prepared them well. In our time together we had many challenges and were always able to find solutions to keep moving forward. In the meantime, before adulthood and for some years after, I became their emotional punching bag. I accepted this role because they did not ask to be put in the situations they were in. I was their role model and protector. I had done the best that I could with what I had, just as my parents and the generations before us had. I was able to empathize with their longing for their biological father because I grew up the same way. This loss of connection grows deep in a person's core. I could relate. I was not aware how much being raised without my biological father affected me, regardless of how toxic he may or may not have been. Just like any parent, I wanted the absolute best that I could afford for my children emotionally and financially. I strived to be the person they needed so that one day they could respect me for my struggles, admire me for my achievements, and be grateful that I was their mom.

I am the first to admit that I wasn't perfect, but I tried. I apologized when the occasion required me to and celebrated their achievements as if they were my own. They each have their own ways of grieving with the loss of the relationship with their father, so I won't say one was more difficult than the other. A huge lesson that I have learned is that you will never understand what someone else is going through because it is their unique journey. Their rebellious attitudes, harsh words that ripped me to my core, judgement, and blame are currently a regular thing even as they are now young adults. Through my healing I learned to forgive my children, my situation, and myself. My strength continued to grow as I learned to set even firmer boundaries with them. I would no longer allow myself to be their punching bag. They needed to learn how to take responsibility for their own actions, just as I had to. I had to protect my mental health so that I could continue to move forward. I constantly remind myself that by continuing to set a positive example and striving to reach my dreams, this regular influence will be part of the ripple effect on them. They are a part of me and my strength and courage will be their superpowers.

The decisions that I made towards my healing have made me stronger, more compassionate, and wiser to my environment and those in it. Being able to forgive Jon has taken a lot of hard work on a few different levels, though I can honestly say from my heart that if he knew better, he would have done better. I know he loves the children, and his decisions are ones that he continues to live with. I also forgive my second ex since I can clearly see his lack of belief in himself. Getting out of his own way would be the greatest gift that he could give to himself. I forgive myself for any decisions that I made due to a mindset of being a victim or having a scarcity mindset. I am so thankful for these lessons that they offered so generously without understanding the depth that they helped me. They could not know, because I did not know. I love that I have been able to grow in ways I never could have imagined for myself.

CHAPTER 10

What is Meant to Be, is Meant to Be

I heard a saying that on average a person has three careers. In my case, the first was working in the hospitality sector, the second was my dental career, and the third was becoming the healer and entrepreneur that I am today. When I became a single parent, I knew that my current position, working with people who had Autism, Down's Syndrome, and Fetal Alcohol Syndrome (F.A.S.), though rewarding, would not cover the bills. I decided to go back to school and finally get a career that Jon had always restricted me from. Thankfully, I did achieve my B.A. and held it closely in my pocket. I opened the career section of the school curriculum guide and dental assisting popped out at me. I considered Law, but my stepdad said that I was "too opinionated". I remember thinking, *a good lawyer needs to be determined to win the case.* I took his advice and thought about becoming a dentist. With three small children, could I do this with the commitment required for school? I decided to settle on becoming an assistant to start to see if it was indeed the avenue I wished to pursue. After all, my priority at the time was to be able to independently support my family as quickly as possible, with minimal amount of strain on everyone. I remembered speaking with the orthodontic assistant in Selkirk, Manitoba that I had when my treatment transpired. As a teenager going through orthodontic treatment catapulted my confidence. This was a career I would enjoy, helping others with finding their smile to gain this same confidence, and it was a professional designation that I would be proud of. My ancestors from the MMF (Manitoba Metis Federation) paid for my courses, textbooks, living expenses, my children's daycare, and travel. I was being handed an opportunity to start a new life! Thank you, ancestors; I will be forever grateful.

I lived, breathed, and slept dental assisting while I cared for my growing family. I would practice tooth positions and names while I helped the children brush and floss. Rather than singing Happy Birthday as some people recommend to get the allotted 2 minutes of oral care necessary for a healthy mouth, an example of my song lyrics were "centrals, laterals, cuspids, bi's," (meaning bicuspids) etc. as I committed myself to the field. My children also learned their teeth names in the process, so it was a win-win. My enthusiasm was contagious in any office I proudly worked in. I was a sponge and soaked up whatever knowledge was given to me. I will admit I was a fish out of water in this profession and very naive. Having good oral hygiene was not something I was raised with, so I ensured my children were very aware of its importance. Teeth became a part of their life as well. I was so grateful to have a professional career that I cleaned the office washroom so the office could save money.

I learned quickly, the option of dentistry always in the back of my mind. I started to realize that I was still struggling too much, so I began paying more attention to things like the scope of practice. Apparently cleaning toilets is not part of it? (Yes, sarcasm is intentional) I had very little self worth, and this was taken advantage of because I had three children at home. Despite being a dental assistant in Manitoba, a registered trained professional, who worked with sharp instruments in a person's mouth, I was barely making ends meet. Thankfully, some offices had become aware of this injustice.

I would learn as much as I could (or wanted to) in one office, then would move on to learning different aspects of the ins and outs of the dental field. I loved orthodontics as I could relate to it so much. It changed my life, and I aimed to do the same for each patient if they wanted it to. Some people were not as excited about getting braces on or having an appliance cemented in their mouth as I had been. I learned to accept this and save my excitement for those who I felt appreciated it. This excitement only grew throughout my career as former patients would stop me in a grocery store or hockey arena, thanking me for helping them change their life. I believed in them just as I had believed in my orthodontist and assistant as a teenager. I provided what so many people lack today: someone who believes in them.

Trying to find the perfect office never happened because I was lost in my own trauma, and I didn't know how to get out. When the divorce was finalized with Jon, I swore subconsciously that I would never let anyone get close to me. He really threw me for a loop. I was so unaware of who I was becoming. I kept pushing down any positive rational emotions, and played the role of the character of who I needed to be in that moment, whether I was at work, home, or out with friends. Helping my fellow assistants became my priority as I soon realized that I needed to learn how to navigate this professional environment quickly if I wanted to live long enough to appreciate any growth in the field. It seemed like few people were courageous enough to take the steps necessary to make a real change. I found it difficult to trust people because I was so blinded by my anger. Resentment and hatred remained sealed under the surface, but it was my fuel to keep doing better as an assistant, human, and mother, and I strived to learn as much as I could. I worked tirelessly as I continued to take one step forward and two steps back. Walls kept coming up that I had to deal with in every aspect of my life. Unfortunately, I couldn't see the people who were genuinely trying to help me, and if I did, I would find an excuse why I couldn't trust them. My journey would have been easier if I was courageous enough to make different choices. My children were always on my mind. It was difficult to distinguish between genuinely authentic people and those who had an ulterior motive. I was stuck in a victim mentality. It makes it feel like everyone is out to get you and no matter what you do, things will never be good enough.

There were some offices that served their patients from the heart, just as I wanted to, and there were others who did not. After about a decade, the anger and resentment that had held me back from healing started to surface. This was not only from my dental career but my whole life at a new level of healing. Patients were always my top priority because they were not aware of what really happened behind the scenes. I will clarify that dental offices are independently owned and operated in Manitoba, and it is the responsibility of the dentist to ensure the by-laws, protocols, and scopes of practice are ethically and morally abided to as per the Hippocratic Oath for their office. The MDA provides the code of ethics and by-laws to ensure, to the best of their ability, that everyone is operating under the same guidelines. Let me put this into perspective for one minute before your imagination starts to take over and your mind fills with unhealthy situations from the internet. Just as any other professional like the police, doctors, lawyers, etc., all of these are people. People are human, and humans can make mistakes. The moral part of this comes down to choice. Every action you do requires some sort of thought process. Some rely on past experiences and some allow a person to venture out and try something new. Either way, being able to take responsibility for your actions signifies the type of person that you are. This is why I became a CBT practitioner (Cognitive Behavior Therapist). It is so easy to blame someone else rather than accept that you made a mistake. My life was full of people who consistently blamed others and chose not to be the better human being because there was always an excuse. It was easier to point their finger at someone else rather than towards themselves. In some cases, like my family where there were so many lies told and half truths, they couldn't keep up anymore. This makes deciphering fact from fiction impossible. The stories that are made up to survive are their reality.

Many assistants were just as innocent, naïve, and feeling the same way as I had, so I took it upon myself to protect them however I could.

I decided to volunteer to be a director on the Manitoba Dental Association Board so that I could help make some real changes that would benefit everyone. I served for six years and brought enthusiasm and passion with me. Did I lose myself? Of course I did; I was very passionate about my career. I am only human, though I learned from a young age to take responsibility for my actions. I did some things that I am not proud of and allowed myself to be bullied for the sake of my career. I became the employee who abided by the office rules regardless of situations I knew to be unethical and thought to be immoral, but I still had my bills and family to support. I did as I was told until one day I had enough.

The experience and knowledge that I acquired by working on the board gave me the confidence to step out from my victim mindset and allowed my voice to be heard. I was raised to do what was right and abide by the law, in this case it was the MDA. After years of being in offices where I was underpaid and often went above and beyond, I had enough. It was easy for me to become emotionally involved in my work because I am an empathetic person and radiate compassion to those around me. I could relate to many of their situations. There were many offices where I worked long hours with overtime, no breaks, and got bullied by others who thought they were in the right. I put up with it simply so I could keep working. These situations developed the thick outer skin that I have today. After my second divorce, I thought I had found my dream job. I was working in a clinic that provided orthodontics and TMJ treatments where I was the head assistant.

Just as tantric has taught me to heal on much deeper levels, my dental career taught me skills that encouraged my strengths like courage and compassion at new levels. I am grateful for the offices that taught me professionalism and business skills as they saw my abilities and appreciated my skills. This next part of my journey summoned a new level of courage that I needed to face my fears, befriend, and forgive to move forward. The case I am referring to was published by

CBC News on June 29, 2018, the Winnipeg Free Press on April 28, 2016, and reported on CTV News on April 29, 2016, regarding how a dentist allowed two employees to provide treatment without licences. As head assistant in this office, I felt it was my responsibility to ensure that the office committed to the high standard of care that it swore to achieve for each patient. I attempted to turn these unethical and immoral actions around by explaining the repercussions to them and encouraged them to get licensed, or to make different decisions to rectify the situation. The employees posing as registered dental assistants did not heed my warnings, nor did the dentist/owner. Rather than do the right thing, the situation only got worse as their confidence built that they "would not get caught." I felt strongly about what was happening because it was right under my nose. I had seen offices be unlawful before and egotistically joke that they would not get caught by the MDA, and this completely downgraded everything that I, as a dental assistant and member of the board, was trying to achieve. I am proud that I was able to help prevent it from continuing. I hope that my actions cause those who know they are guilty to stop and think twice. I believe in Karma, and the universe will provide what it needs to direct people on the right path if they are willing. This is the path I have chosen for decades.

As per CBC News, the dentist "...agreed to a 4 ½ month suspension, as well as audits by the dental association over the next two years to ensure his compliance." He must "also take courses in record keeping, jurisprudence and ethics, as well as to cover some of his costs related to the case."

I am grateful for those offices who showed me the darker side of the profession, and I saw distinct evidence of the battle that the MDA was up against, though from a different angle. Like someone knowingly running a red light while driving, the police cannot be everywhere all the time and a negligent driver could kill someone. Many people are fearful of coming forward and reporting to the MDA due to the repercussions on themselves and their families. Personally, I nearly lost my house. I knew once the doctor found out that I reported him I would lose my job. I chose to help the MDA because after my second divorce, and my lifelong battle with people taking advantage of their position, I had enough. Everyone, the public and I, deserved so much better. The MDA did keep my name confidential, and throughout the process they were extremely supportive. I was confident that I could find another position, which was part of the reason I helped as much as I did.

Even when I doubted the integrity of those in my profession, the underlying faith is what got me through. At one point in my career someone reported me for going beyond my scope of practice. As a relatively new assistant I was overwhelmed and wanted to do the best job I could. As a single parent, who was solely responsible to raise my children, the financial obligations never seemed to end. Wages, as with other professions, have always been a concern for assistants. The hierarchy that prevails is understood, though treating each office independently with their unique team environment only promotes equality on the surface. This was not the reality in many offices. The bitterness and resentment grew inside of me as I was encouraged and at times told to go beyond my scope if I wanted to keep my job. As dental assistants in Manitoba we are protected by the dentist with their malpractice insurance. I got tired of fighting and trying to find the perfect office, so I again did what I was told until I was careless, probably wanting to be caught so that this circus could end and I could take a stand as I represented all dental assistants. Understand, when you go through something as intense as the Peer Review Committee, ALL your thoughts and feelings resurface of not being good enough. The truth of what happened, all the decades of abuse and bullying in the workplace, were surfacing. I am so proud of my dental community and the steps that they have taken in attempting to stop those who make the choices they do. I truly believe in Karma, and she is an amazing, wonderful woman who truly does "get her man," and/or woman in this case. This is what happened in my case - others who have been through the process had their own journey. I am hoping others will look in the mirror and find their inner strength to comply with their scope of practice and for the employers to treat their employees how they deserve to be treated. This is why I have become a coach, a CBT practitioner.

I realize that even though I have a flag on my license, I can now wear this like a badge of honor. It has been a long road to get to this point with lots and lots of reflection and healing. To do this, I surrendered my license, left the field, and my respected position on the board. Only one person knew how this hit me like a brick wall when it was time for the next meeting. I sat down and cried like a baby. All the anger, resentment, feelings of disrespect, and lack of integrity to myself surfaced as it poured out of me. There were many feelings that I had pushed down throughout my life that I was not only unaware of, but also did not know how to process. This included family, professionals, employers, friends, spouses, and me. What I also realised was that I had to forgive myself for all those years that I felt backed into a corner without a voice or taken seriously because of my situation. As an adult, I always had the choice to do differently. I was either unaware, scared, or lacked confidence in myself. NOW, I thank the person who reported me. It shook up the world that I needed to have shaken up. It gave me the wake-up call that I needed, and I heard it loud and clear. I found out who I am completely. Tantric has taught me how to raise and process these emotions so that I could become a vibrational match to live the life I want.

I love the dental community with all my heart. I gave back as much as I was able by volunteering as the "Tooth Fairy" and on a mission trip to Africa where our team helped 672 children. It is an amazing place with many compassionate people. There were people who saw my potential and believed in me when I most needed it despite me not believing in myself, and I forgive others for their ethical and moral mistakes as I know everyone is going through their own journey and I can relate. I am grateful for all who have been a part of my dental journey and I keep their knowledge close to my heart.

CHAPTER 11

Becoming an Alchemist

There were so many necessary changes in my life. I knew significant change was needed, though I did not know what this looked like, when the changes would happen, where I would be mentally, emotionally, and physically, or how this change would happen. The biggest part of becoming an alchemist is your faith. I knew that I could achieve whatever I put my mind to. With the children all graduated from high school, I allowed myself to surrender to whoever was protecting and guiding me once again. I had worked hard to ensure that my children were prepared for adulthood to the best of my abilities, knowing that my guidance and support was in reach if they needed me. I never believed in empty nest syndrome until it happened to me. It allowed me to take a hard look at myself in the mirror as an overprotective, single parent. Due to the abandonment I never realized how territorial I was over my children. I never wanted them to feel what I had. This was part of looking in my mirror. The short-lived relationships that I had were never right. I continued to search for the father figure, or love, that I lacked throughout my life. I was confused and I knew this was my opportunity to finally find out who I was!

As a parent you quickly learn that your children do not come with a manual. I did everything in my power to give my children a better life than I had, and I attempted to protect them from the terrible situations that I ended up in. I encouraged them to learn from my mistakes. Though like my mom, I had unintentionally passed the ancestral limiting beliefs and trauma from us to them. Simply by being with my family at functions, daily living, parenting styles, and even habits. Traits that were held in high regard in the family were all dissolving after my maternal grandparents passed away. I did not know what a limiting belief was because as an adult I tried to do what I thought was right. I didn't feel limited.

I started by going back to square one with focusing on my health. What I needed to do to accept where I was in life. If this was how I was supposed to live it, then I needed to allow myself to accept the hand I was dealt. I had no idea what I was in store for, only intuitively I knew I was meant to do so much more than I had been up until this point. I joined an online fitness group that taught me a whole different way of eating, exercising, and meditating. I had never meditated before. In church we had prayed, but this was very different. I liked the way it calmed my monkey brain down. I was able to think and focus in a very different way. Over the last ten years I had also set firmer boundaries with people who I allowed into my heart. I was tired of the dating games people played and the lies that they told. I often wondered, why can't people be themselves? Then I realized that I didn't know who I was anymore. Robin Sharma's *Leader Without a Title* changed my world. My children had defined me as their mother, I was known as the treasurer for the MDAA Board, I was known as the PAC President to many of the people where my children went to school, and I was a dental assistant who could be relied on to get things done. Who was I inside? I still did not have these answers.

I joined a genealogy site that gave me a lot of answers regarding my paternal family, including that I was too late to meet my dad. He had passed away in 2008, physically paralyzed and alone, living his last days in a hospice after a brutal home invasion many years earlier. I learned that he had a hard life. My mom was protecting me from the many poor decisions he continually made during his life. I wear my heart on my sleeve, and I would have been no different with him. She knew me well, though it would have been nice to have the choice. Something told me that my mom would not be untruthful about who my dad was. We did three cheek swabs and they all said that we were not related. I was beyond disappointed, though something kept encouraging me to do more. *Think outside the box Pauline. You can do this!* I wracked my brain, then finally allowed my navigational skills to shine. Shine they did! The fourth test we did was a saliva test.

In December 2022, fifty-one years after I was born, I received the scientific evidence to show that Bev, my cousin, and I are paternal first cousins because Ted Aguesse was my dad! We sensed it the moment we met, but I had been misguided so many times in this regard that I needed proof. Many of my personality traits were like my paternal side. I am entrepreneurial and physically we have the same lazy eye and nose. I got my auburn hair and height from my dad. From the stories that I heard about my dad's family, my grandmother and I would have gotten along well. Our no nonsense, hard working, resourceful traits are similar. When I think about my mom keeping this information from me for so long despite how similar I was to them, I realize I must have driven her insane some days. I can be very determined when I need to be and this was one of those cases. Having the ability to believe in something this fierce told me that I did have faith in myself. I wasn't sure who I believed in, God, the Universe, Buddha? Whoever was listening, I could feel someone, maybe an angel, protecting me somehow. Having a scientific mind, I had turned my back on religion. It had not proved to help me in the past, as far as I knew. It was hard to believe in anything when I did not believe in myself fully. Even though I knew who my dad was, this still did not make me feel completely whole.

My world was changing drastically, and I had to be firm with myself as well as those around me. I had to set firm boundaries with family and people who I thought were friends - everyone who was trying to hold me back. I now represented their fears and feelings that they refused to face. By getting rid of the toxicity in my life, even though it was extremely hard, I felt lighter. Over the next few years, I slowly managed to get rid of as much drama as I could. This included no longer allowing my children to treat me as a punching bag. It was time for them to face their own fears and take responsibility for their own lives. I could no longer do it for them.

Father's Day has always been uncomfortable for me. I have always had stepdads, not a biological father. The bond between biological parents and their offspring is so much stronger than I realized, and it affects decisions, daily focus, habits, and overall characteristics that we may inherit. Throughout my life I have tried to ignore that he wasn't in my life, and I could have pretended that I was okay with it. The part that consistently made my days a challenge were the constant reminders that he was not around. The undercurrents of limiting beliefs were so strong that my dad could no longer fight them, so he left. I was left empty for 51 years as part of me stayed hidden. He had a choice. My mom had a choice. I did not. That choice was taken from me, along with part of my identity. Every time I had to state my last name, I felt the sting of the reminder. My last name changed four times in my life: Einarson, Simundson, Danilis, and Grouette, adding to the feeling of not being whole. Knowing that Aguesse is my true, paternal and maiden name filled the empty spot where part of my heart was meant to go for my whole life. I finally felt like I knew where I belonged. To heal past ancestors, I have committed to this tantric journey and have become an alchemist so that it may be lighter and less intense for my children. Jon's relationships with his children are still possible while he is alive. Is there some anger here? Not really, only a lot of disappointment in the potential of what the relationships could have been. One day I can only hope that he will see how wonderful the children are rather than choosing to remain in his own victim mindset.

On Father's Day, 2023, I am committing this day to my biological father, Theodore Alexander Aguesse, knowing that he will always be with me in spirit and love in my heart. I have done DNA tests where people tried to say he was not biologically my dad, though my heart told me differently. Well-known physicist Albert Einstein states his definition of insanity is "endlessly repeating the same process and hoping for a different result." I will admit I may be insane at times, though I know I am able to come out of it quicker than before. The testing process was a roller coaster of emotions for me and the few people around me who I confided in. I was so sure of my paternity that I agreed to have my story told as an episode in a TV series called *Secrets, Lies and DNA Ties*. This aired on April 6, 2023. The results on the show were the second test that I did which was a cheek swab. I realize that my case was different because the cheek swab was from my first cousin, not Ted himself, since he has passed on. I agreed to do the TV show in hopes that my paternal family would surface and show to those who I had contacted and did not believe me that I knew deep in my soul that we were related. People join genealogy searches for numerous reasons; loneliness, wanting to prey on those vulnerable emotions, interest in reconnecting with family, or those like me who need concrete answers about where they came from. With this book, I am hoping that paternal relatives will contact me so I can continue to break our traumatic, familial chains and forge a new path for generations to come.

Being able to get to know my first paternal cousin has been instrumental in my research. Besides being very patient with the four tests we did together, she has shared some stories, provided answers, and filled gaps in part of the story that my mom told me. The puzzle pieces not only fit together, but she was also positive, deep in her soul, that we were related from the moment we met. Her encouragement made it easy to befriend fear and look it in the eye. Fear, worry, doubt, and loneliness would no longer control my actions. After taking many more coach related courses for my healing, for my business, and ultimately so that I can serve clients on a much deeper level, I know my purpose: helping men and women who grew up without a biological parent so they can feel whole. When I got the answer I needed to feel whole, a calm came over me and I could focus on healing past generations and those to come. By continuing to help others, my life will continue to reach new heights as I continue to surpass each goal I set. This is Karma.

What was my purpose? Helping everyone around me and sacrificing my needs was always the norm. It was time for me to start on my bucket list. What did I truly want? I knew my current career as a dental assistant was not going to get me to a "living the dream" type of life. I could feel deeply that my life was meant for more, or why else would I have been saved so many times? There have been unexplained times in my life that should have had different outcomes. I have had numerous car accidents in my life, and I have never broken a bone, yet I am quite clumsy. In 2014, I was rear-ended by a semi truck carrying water, causing it to hit me twice as the water in the holding tank shifted the weight of the truck back and forth. I was on the city perimeter, and the driver was not paying attention to the accident that occurred about a kilometer ahead of us. I, and the other two cars ahead of me, were able to stop, but he hit me at approximately eighty kilometers an hour. I thought for sure I was dead this time as flashes of my children ran through my mind. I saw white! I walked away without a scratch. The universe always has my back. That was the last car accident that I was in. The white light told me that it was not my time. I have work to do while I am still on Earth.

I realized that I would have to take some courses for an upgrade, or I had to change fields altogether. In university I had always been interested in psychology and what makes us tick, or in other words, why people do the things they do. Part of the new journey was to heal my old wounds that kept touching the surface. Cognitive Behavior Therapy (CBT) was a great fit as it also helped me set firmer boundaries with men and people who were not destined to be in my life anymore. There is a saying that people come into your life for a reason, a season, or a lifetime. I heard this from a colleague, and it rang loud and true for me, so it stuck as one of my favorite quotes. CBT increased my confidence in many areas of my life, especially at work. I started to develop confidence and self worth. Though it was still in its infancy, the difference was drastic. The changes felt like I was going in the right direction, so I kept taking actions that I gravitated towards. They felt different, but good different. The year 2017 changed my life in ways that I never thought possible.

In 2017, Robin came into my life after I surrendered. When I talk about surrendering, I mean literally giving up any kind of searching for a partner. This included online dating sites as I forced the idea of looking for someone out of my mind. I had been thinking about it for a while and contemplated every alternative. What if someone was interested and I didn't notice because I was in this new mindset? It really didn't matter anymore. I would be okay living by myself with a couple pets to keep me company. Surrendering was one of the best things I did for myself. This was the beginning of many significant changes. On my first date with Robin I laid all my cards on the table; finances, divorces, children, and I told him I expected the same from him if there was any chance for a second date. We stayed until the restaurant closed as time zoomed by. Change was scary but it felt good! I committed to making more changes in every part of my life. With a newfound support system, my husband (married 2019) and mother-in-law, I was able to initiate the steps required to start on a new and very different healing journey. They believed in me. I met my soulmate who loved me for who I am, believed in me, and supported my purpose, part of which was finding my paternal family. With the kids figuring out their own paths, now was the time to start living for me. My heart was slowly filling up; now I needed to fill my soul.

Without prior knowledge, we bought and moved onto land that was farmed and inhabited by our ancestors south of Winnipeg. I believe everything happens for a reason. We moved just as COVID-19 started.

I was laid off for three months, so I started to read real self help books that were in alignment with the health group I was still active in. Next came Sharma's *5AM Club* which helped me revamp my schedule, incorporate my new exercises, healthy eating, and meditation which I added to my daily journaling. He has a ninety-day challenge which I found myself able to do because I was focused and determined to create a new life for my family and any grandchildren that may come along. Once Robin and I moved, Jay Shetty's Coaching course kept coming up in my news feed. I had always liked psychology, so I discussed this option with Robin and he saw the benefits of me becoming a coach. I signed up with the Jay Shetty Certification School (JSCS). There were feelings of guilt rising because we just purchased our dream property and were creating our dream home. Did I want to open this Pandora's box when everything was going so well? All the limiting beliefs of not being good enough, that I don't really deserve to be this happy because no one else looks as satisfied and content with their life, surfaced. Who do I think I am? Major imposter syndrome and having an unsupportive family only reinforced this, but I had Robin and his mom. "You only live once" and "you won't know unless you try," she would say. I healed so many old wounds properly because I thought, *if I am opening this box, I am opening it wide open!*

After I graduated I felt like I still had my whole life ahead of me. I was confident and determined to establish myself as well as I knew how. Like an onion, I had multiple layers to work through to reach each level of healing that goes beyond the outer peel, reconnecting with the inner child and ancestors on a spiritual level, a supra conscious level. I needed to energetically view each situation with a bird's-eye-view from above. Each level may consist of similar topics as the previous one, the difference is the perspective and ability to heal faster due to familiarity and confidence that we can do it again. Another way to look at it is going up a staircase. Each one is a new step but we are familiar with the height and width of each step so we are confident that we can take that step again. If we wobble and need to land on the previous step, that's okay, we are human and can stabilize ourselves, as I had already experienced. We have many areas that comprise our life: family, health, faith, career, finances, etc. Prioritizing where I wanted to start was easy-I wanted a new career. I started to take the necessary steps that I needed to for myself. I was back at the dental office, but I felt like I was not valuing my time. At school, I made amazing friends from all over the world. The fact that I could talk to people from totally different cultures was amazing. This was a hard concept for me to wrap my head around, though I was excited about the prospects. I was now influencing, guiding, and talking to people from all over the world on a daily basis. This blew my mind. My heart was now elsewhere, no longer at the office. Initially, many hard feelings came up. There was a lot of anger and resentment coming up that I had pushed down for decades. So much so that it scared me sometimes. I didn't know where it was coming from. I realized that I had to leave the dental field.

In April 2022, I officially gave up my license and resigned from the board. I needed a clean break to sort myself out. This drastic change was necessary to heal, come to peace, and allow myself to move forward from decades of trauma, stemming from even before I was born. I had to surrender everything, my family, friends, children, and career, to heal through the deep layers that haunted me. I have learned that the more I heal myself, the more I will be able to relate and guide others, because I have done it and put my faith in the universe and Karma. My sacrifices paved the way for more creative genius to flourish and provide for others worldwide. In 2022, Guided Journey Coaching and Dental Consulting was born. While serving clients 1:1 and conducting group coaching, I became a Certified Vision Board Facilitator and a two-time, #1 best-selling co-author of collaborations that initiated my ascent to greatness. By opening the door of my story, I know others will follow. These opportunities were presented to me by the universe. I accepted because I knew the universe always has my back!

My life changed that day. I no longer took life for granted and committed to make changes that would be everlasting. I did not know what these looked like or how they would happen; I only knew that I needed to take action to initiate them to be sustainable for others. There have been many times I was guided closer and closer to the town where my dad's family grew up to get the answers I needed to feel whole. Many times, when I felt backed into a corner and could not find a solution, one presented itself in some shape or form. Financially, I was barely able to make ends meet, though there was always a way to get through whatever the situation was. Whether this was being able to qualify for subsidy so that my children could play sports, or Legal Aid finding out where Jon worked so that they could garnish his paychecks to feed his children. Being able to be aware of the signs helped me to understand how gifted I am. I was given this gift from my maternal side. After the semi truck accident, my mom called and asked where I was. I was laying in the hospital bed waiting to be released. This is standard protocol after such an intense accident. The many times when there were those feelings of red flags, that was my inner soul trying to guide me. I was not as receptive back then because I wanted to give everyone the benefit of the doubt. I didn't want people to be mad at me so I would do what they needed. I believe that our dreams hold messages even at a young age. Meditation taught me to calm myself through breathwork and to be okay being still.

I have always taken little bits of knowledge from different sources and created what I thought to be an all encompassing and accurate synapsis of a goal for me. As with coaching, at one point I worked with three different coaches for different areas of my life. For accountability I had a business coach, I was coached in alchemy for myself to trust and decipher parts of myself from a bird's-eye-view (AKA the superconscious), and for deep spiritual reconnection (so I could give my ancestors peace and the ability to break the limitations holding back our family) I worked with my tantric shaman. I pride myself on having the ability to see situations from different angles. Working with a good coach will empower you to reach your destination faster because they can relate to your experience. As everyone has their own journey, trusting in possible outcomes and avoiding the hardships will ensure that you can live your best life. Though, only you can do the hard work that is required. No one can do it for you.

For me, a combination of alchemy teachings and tantric healing have allowed me to experience the renaissance required to feel whole. I would find parts of both to be comprehensive so that I was able to dissect, understand, and heal what I needed so I could move forward. In theory, alchemy is having the ability to turn lead into gold. Lead representing the trauma, divorce, depression, suicidal ideologies, and deep inner need to discover myself. The gold represents the renaissance in all its magnificence. In a spiritual sense, it is healing and providing peace to our ancestors so that you and I can create a renaissance within ourselves. This deep work with my inner child radiates with whomever I speak to and will affect the future generations. In a simpler form, accepting that we don't know what we don't know and allowing ourselves to become aware of signs that the Universe provides is part of tantric. Understanding the undercurrents that cause shifts all around us daily only comes from doing the deep inner work.

Mom and dads' spirits acted as the wall to break the ancestral chains while my tantric shaman was my vessel that held the safe space so that I could bring our maternal and paternal ancestors' forgiveness, peace, gratitude, and love. The generations of religious and societal trauma do not have to exist. While my mom and biological dad shared this plane of being, coming together to work as one was not achievable. My hard work and guidance have allowed them to lay to rest all the hatred, fear, resentment, and anger that they held towards each other, and over time they will be at peace.

My 7 stages of Alchemy:

1. **Calcination**- This is allowing ourselves to get out of our own way of achieving happiness. I used to consider myself a perfectionist and took pride in this, especially being in the dental field. I first had to prioritize my goals into categories like family, career, finances, health, spirituality, relationships, and extracurriculars/hobbies. After taking a positive intelligence course I realized that my worst enemy is judgement. It is everywhere, and society only perpetuates it. Perfectionism brings out the ego, fears, self-sabotage behaviors, etc. I had to be brutally honest with myself in order to become my authentic self.

2. **Dissolution**- This involves developing a sense of oneself so that I could develop a sense of spiritual maturity. I am very grateful for a colleague who is also a minister because we had a brutally honest conversation about God. I had a lot of anger in me still at this point and many questions that I needed answered. Being born into a Roman Catholic family and being told repeatedly that "God will only give you what you can handle," I had enough! How much more did I need to absorb and endure to free myself from the trauma I experienced? The divorces, perfectionism, loss of jobs, death of my grandparents, and more. The colleague was so patient and kind. He sat and listened; I had warned him before that I had a lot of anger and that I needed to come to some sort of resolution. He understood with no judgement, only respect for helping me free myself from my own fears, self-doubt, and pride. I had to take responsibility for my own part in all these situations. Rather than facing some of these extremely hard truths some people turn to alcohol, drugs, gambling, workaholism, and other addictions like social media so that they can avoid reality. At one point, going to my child's hockey practice with a rye and coke in a coffee travel mug was my thing. I am grateful that this was short-lived as I realized there was a problem.

3. **Separation**- This is forgiveness of others - the many toxic friendships and family members taking advantage of your empathetic ways. I had to dissect my true feelings in situations and stop sweeping them under the rug. I had to accept how angry I was, and this was difficult because there were a lot of suppressed feelings! While I meditated, I imagined two boxes; one was full of unprocessed emotions and the other held emotions that I investigated with brutal honesty no matter how angry, sad, resentful, or whichever emotion needed to be processed, and placed it in this box. It worked. Once each emotion was worked through, I was able to move on. I wrote letters to those I needed to separate from emotionally. I did not send them, but I would have a fire and burn the letter as a form of processing, so universally the message would get to the person if they wanted to have a relationship with me. This may sound like I am avoiding conflict, but no, this is Karma and the universe working in conjunction, in your favor. This is also a way to reconnect with your inner child. Rebuilding the relationship so that it is respectful, allowing her in on my daily decisions so she never feels alone again.

4. **Conjunction**-This is learning to forgive myself. All those times that I pushed aside better judgement because life pressures took over and 90% of rational thought was gone. I have had a few of those moments for sure. This is learning to look in that mirror honestly. Accepting the good and not very proud moments as well. Giving yourself a bit of grace and accepting that you are human, and you are living the way you know how, for the moment. Life has a way of giving you more chances to improve on these moments so forgive yourself. This will not happen instantly and learning how much grace to give yourself is also important.

Part of learning to be your authentic self is stepping into each emotion for the circumstance and asking yourself:

- What did I like/not like about _____?
- What could I have done differently so I would have had a better outcome?
- What made me make the decision that I did?

5. **Fermentation**- At this stage your sense of reality has been shattered. I began literally ridding myself of anything that was toxic, looking at the relationships objectively, and deciding how I feel when I am with a certain person, how I feel when they come into my mind. If you are unsure, it would be safe to assume that there is a reason your mind is trying to protect you. Think of shedding the person from your life or if it is impossible, establishing firmer boundaries. At this stage learning how to understand the messages your body is giving you is part of your authenticity. This will take time so don't rush. Give yourself some time to heal, which is like giving your body space. Another way to rid yourself of toxic energy in your living area is to purge. Any material object that brings a negative thought to your mind should be given away, sold, or thrown out. This will provide a new perspective or clarity so that new ideas can come to you and help add positive space to your spiritual body.

This is a painful plunge into your past. Usually this involves many blocks of things that your mind was protecting you from. For example, for me the abuse and trauma from my marriage took an enormous amount of work to feel those feelings again. I never wanted to think about them again, but I forced myself to heal the past and not stay stuck.

This is like a spiritual detox, like I had with my coach about God, which is necessary before enlightenment can happen. This can be a very complicated journey so many people separate it into two parts:

1. **Putrefaction**- This is when you start to create your new story and decide which part of the present story is fact or fiction.

What helped me for this part was acquiring new information about my dad. I had been living my mom's old story that was full of untruths because she could not tell the difference anymore regarding which story was hers and which one was the old one passed on from ancestors, who brought along limiting beliefs.

2. **Spiritization**- When you start to look at the world through a new lens and start to trust your intuition. This is not just having thoughts that come into our heads, but acting on those thoughts so we learn to trust ourselves.

It can be easy to fall into a depression at this point which is why it is important to work with a trained, certified coach to guide you through to the other side. It becomes easier to let go of the attachment of material items, relationships, and self-victimization.

6. **Distillation**- This is a stage of integrating all our spiritual realizations into our lives for them to become permanent on a much deeper level of healing within ourselves. This is a strong transformation of peace and inner bliss within us. Examples in my life of this are when I was reunited with Stephan, my miscarried son, and my paternal family who watch over him for me in their world. Another time during a tantric meditation, I was reunited with my aboriginal ancestors. I learned to respect their guidance on a different level, so I was also able to love them and forgive them differently than I ever had before. This is enlightenment or self-realization.

7. **Coagulation**- This is when you are finally able to break free from your mind and connect to a higher consciousness or soul. For me this is when I speak to Mother Universe directly. This is a meeting point between two opposites like the Ying and the Yang, black and white, or Heaven and Hell - self-awareness without duality. The physical

universe is not separate from our mind, body, soul, or spiritual reality. Much of the judgement we feel from others is only the insecurity within ourselves.

I know that I am a great coach not only because I am able to relate to others, but because I have been there. Each situation is our mirror. I have noticed my judgemental patterns so I can understand more clearly where the judgement is coming from. This is how I have been able to break the cycle and move past the pattern to understand that every experience, situation, and person is a mirror of what we are projecting.

I have learned that we are all here to learn something from one another. Every person you meet is meant to show you something different about yourself. Seeing yourself in others gives you compassion, patience, strength, and love.

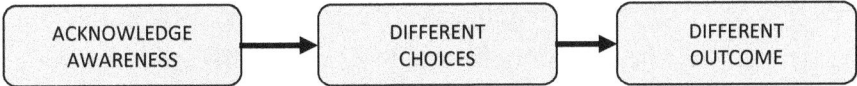

ACKNOWLEDGE AWARENESS	→	DIFFERENT CHOICES	→	DIFFERENT OUTCOME

Perspective is a two-way street; when you judge others you are giving them permission to judge you too. Alternatively, when you shine your light, you give others permission to shine theirs.

I want to reiterate that these stages were what I felt best described my journey. Be mindful that everyone is unique and special in their own way. It may feel at times that you are taking two steps forward and one step back. This will be different for everyone. I was determined to get answers, so I was very bold. I stepped out of my comfort zone in all areas of my life. Be patient with yourself, forgive, and love.

CHAPTER 12

Healing and Growing Beyond Imagination!

Ahuge part of my healing journey includes the tantric journey with my Tantric Shaman, Amba Kahly. We met each other at JCSC. Part of the curriculum is to provide complimentary coaching sessions to fellow coaches before they let us out into the real world. Amba comes from a long line of tantric shamans - five to be exact. When I saw her post about looking for clients, I was at the point in my journey where I had been able to connect with my dad through meditation, but I wanted concrete answers now. I was scared because I didn't know what to expect. Since I am not the tantric, I am not going to try to explain what she does. All I know is that she acts as a safe vessel so that the universal energy from the mother can pass through to the spiritual plane so I could heal past blocked trauma's. We push each other to keep getting stronger, and I would not have gotten to where I am so quickly if it wasn't for her guidance and support. In my mind I had committed to doing the inner work by becoming a coach by already having been through counselling, reading self-help books, and listening to podcasts. There are coaches out there who are not certified, so beware. Amba will be the first to caution you to only work with someone you know that you can completely trust. This is our relationship. Sometimes during part of the meditation the client is going deep into a hypnosis state to break down the high brick walls that have formed from centuries of generational trauma. The tantric acts as a safe vessel that connects the masculine and feminine energies to become one. These can be lost souls as when I connected with Stephan.

Meditation has taught and encouraged me to expand my inner strength by first creating a foundation. In 2017 when I first started meditating, there was a group of ladies that I connected with from the fitness group. This was a side group that was created to offer daily meditations with people who we trusted and wanted to get to know on a more personal level. This daily meditation guided me towards connecting with my dad on a spiritual level. With the lady who headed the group, I was able to connect with my dad in his hospital room on his last days and tell him what I needed to say. Spiritually he also surrendered to me on another occasion, as he apologized for not being part of my life. He kneeled in front of me, as if to serve me with much respect. He vowed to make up for it. For those of you who don't believe in ghosts or spirits, you may think this is a bunch of phoney bologna. All I can say is that if I had not experienced it myself, I would not believe it either. If you think of it like a puzzle and become aware of signs that the universe, God, Buddha, or whoever you believe in is sending you, it does make sense. A huge part of this comes with surrendering yourself so that you let go and stop fighting. Not being in control is very scary and real; I understand, I have been there. I have also surrendered and know how much more peaceful, grounded, and calm I feel. It is so much better than the anger, angst, and all those negative feelings I used to put on myself. Understanding the different levels of consciousness and planes are my new reality.

I had experience with spirits, or ghosts, a few times before in my life, though I didn't understand they were signs. In Whitemouth, the hotel was over one hundred years old. I would often hear noises coming from the attic. There was a door that went up there with a staircase. I had my younger sister with me so I know I was not dreaming. There was an old man with a cat sitting on the steps. We ran back to our bedroom in fear. Another time in the Ste. Agathe hotel a politician was living in one of our rooms. He was going through a terrible divorce and one night he killed himself. I had served him on many occasions and we got to know each other while he was alive. My sibling and I would place our shoes between our beds at the head neatly before we went to sleep so we could find them the next day. We had an apartment that was part of the hotel as living quarters and the restaurant was just through a door from our living room. I woke one night as I could hear the sound of a cup being placed on a saucer; somehow, I knew it was him. Soon after a mist of a little girl came into our room and started trying on our shoes. He opened the door to signal the child that it was time to go. She left and from then on whenever I had someone stay over, he would pop his head in to be sure I was okay. It became comforting knowing this male figure was watching over me. Besides family, my latest encounter was with relatives from the current house we are living in. They were the original owners and the family stayed in the house until we bought it. During the first few weeks around 11PM -1AM I would hear voices visiting as they played cards and had a few drinks. I was losing sleep and it was starting to become a habit. I told a lady from the meditation group about them, and she told me to let them know that I needed my sleep because I had to get up for work the next day. As simple, and silly, as this sounded I did it and they have never returned.

While I was learning how to connect with my dad and some family members, comforting things would happen to let me know he was around. Robin was working away from home, so I allowed this opportunity to focus on healing and connecting. We have a long driveway and are required to leave our garbage cans at the end to get picked up. I put the cans laying down in the back of the truck, drove to the house, and proceeded on with my evening. I was tired so I left the cans in the back and I could hear his heavy footsteps on the porch. My dad stood the cans up telling me to take them out before I forgot about them. It took me a few of his visits to truly know that he was with me. This was new for me, and I would never know how tall he was, what he smelled like, or what his voice sounded like. I would never be or know what it felt like to be "Daddy's Little Girl." This longing to know him more was raw, and I had to start living again. Wanting to connect was starting to consume me. After about a year of working together, a big milestone we achieved was discovering our spirit animals.

We are very outdoor type of people and I believe in the power of Mother Nature and her wisdom. My dad's spirit animal is a bald eagle. My mom and I took a walk by the river near our house and dad, as an eagle, was there. I just said "Hi," but my mom surprised me. She was mesmerized as she stared at the eagle. Did she know this was dad's spirit animal? She never did tell me, but I had to call her three times before she broke her trance. It was like they were talking. I asked her what she was doing, and she said she always liked bald eagles and watching them, so graceful with their wide wingspans. My aunt had told me one time that Ted never got married because there was a girl who stole his heart, and that his family would not let them be together. He went into a deep depression, made a lot of bad choices, and you know the rest of his story. I wonder if this girl was my mom. There are some things I may never find out.

My spirit animal is a buck which symbolizes strength, stamina, maturity, instinct, regeneration, grace, and spiritual enlightenment. He wears his antlers like a crown representing nobility and leadership. Today I can relate to the buck in a way that brings me peace. During a meditation, I was in a field with forests surrounding it. At one point the whole treeline was full of does (female deer) standing shoulder to shoulder, then a large, very regal buck appeared walking to the front of the line, stopped, and looked on towards me. I remember thinking, *Is this supposed to be me? How am I supposed to relate to him? He is so strong, and everyone automatically looks to him for guidance.* He walked to me, never breaking eye contact. I was not intimidated. I was grateful for the support and wisdom by his grace and knowledge. I put my hand on his back, and we walked together to another part of the forest as the others looked on. Over time the bond between us grew as we became one. It was a very powerful meditation because it represented me. I knew I needed to work on my confidence because this was part of my dad that kept him away. Whenever I would feel weak, my buck would come into my mind and I would feel better, more confident that I could take the actions necessary to move forward and achieve whatever I wanted to.

The first year working with Amba Kahly was full of awareness and connection as I started to take steps that I never dreamed possible before. Retiring my dental license, becoming a #1 best selling co-author twice, becoming a Certified Awareness Coach, CBT practitioner, and Vision Board Facilitator all in one year and filming the television show regarding my paternity! I let the world know that I was serious, and people would know who I was. At one point in my life, I had a business making sport's guards (2011-13). I was going through my second divorce, flying by the seat of my pants and it grew too fast for one person because I was still working full-time. When I sold it, it felt like I dodged a bullet. Success was a real fear. All the imposter syndrome feelings rose again. Other than my hotel experience I had never taken a business course for guidance. This time was different. I did it before; I learned from my mistakes by ensuring I had the time, knowledge, and resources at my disposal to make it successful. I was confident I could do it again! Deep inside I still longed to find a paternal family, though it was different now. As I surrendered to the universe, pieces started to fall into place. I started my new business, Guided Journey Coaching and Consulting, with a firm foundation in place.

Part of the confidence came from learning about who I was, authentically to my core. I was still doing research with the genealogy group, though I started to feel like I needed to be more creative to get the answers I required to feel whole. I researched online and was on the phone for hours getting little tidbits of information here and there. Every small piece of information felt like I hit a golden nugget! I found that my dad grew up in Deerhorn, near Eriksdale and I was able to locate where he was buried - Abbeville Cemetery. This was a huge breakthrough! When I finally found the cemetery, not only did I find my dad, the rest of my family was there too. I had been looking for them my whole life. I broke down as I felt I wanted to melt like snow into the Earth to be with them. At this point I still did not have the scientific evidence that we were related. I was following my instincts and working intensely with Amba Kahly. Yes, I would say I became consumed with finding out who I was. Robin was supportive throughout my journey as he saw how important it was for me to know who I am. How was I supposed to move forward when it felt like only half of me was going forward? I needed to know my other half so that I could take action and move forward as a whole being. It did not make sense to go forth halfway. I did this my whole life, and the challenges, though great, were necessary to build my strength, but I felt beyond that now. My drive to find answers was so strong, my dad's spirit was with me a few times a week. I would wake up in the morning and feel him sitting at my dining room table having coffee and reading the paper. It sounds crazy but it brought me comfort knowing he was there. I would hear his footsteps on the porch. There was a bald eagle that started hanging around our property, which I knew now to be him watching on from above. With my alchemy training I know this to be like the superconscious. I developed this bird's-eye-view to understand different areas of my life as I continued to heal the pain and developed strength and confidence. For most of my life I had committed to becoming a better person for my children, and now I looked forward to meeting my dad's family.

At one point I had done so much research and the pull was so strong to find and meet my paternal family that I collapsed. I wanted to bring some of dad's dirt back home with me so that I could be with him on a daily basis. The amazing thing about working with Amba Kahly is that she is like a psychic. She knew I wasn't ready to transfer soil. This was a very heavy, dangerous thing to do and she had warned me to wait, but I am not a patient person. I felt like I had waited long enough. A day came to me in the winter of 2022. The trip would take about a two-and-a-half-hour drive. I had a small shovel, a bag for the dirt, and a letter like the one I would have written when I was twenty so I could leave it on his grave. Someone had been looking after his grave and I wanted to know who because I am sure they would have more answers to what kind of a person he was. Even if they found the letter, I would leave my contact information in another plastic bag to protect it from the elements in hopes they would contact me. Dad, spiritually, agreed with Amba that this was not the time.

It was spring thaw with some snow still on the ground and I had been waiting very patiently all winter for the ground to thaw so I could bring some of my dad home. All I wanted was to see him, talk to him, and be with him. I would only need a small shovel of dirt. I had everything packed on the counter so I wouldn't forget anything over the long drive. Robin recommended that I use the truck because it was icy, the wind was blowing, it was snowing a little, and probably not the best conditions to be driving down one of Manitoba's best-known highways for accidents. Robin has learned to let me do what I need to feel whole. He trusted my judgement and would not interfere trying to keep me away from my paternal family because I would hold it against him. I needed this deep in my soul. Looking back, was this a little reckless? Yes, though so had other parts of my life been. I could get there even if I had to drive a little slower and, in the worst-case scenario, I had friends along the way that I could stay with until the weather cleared up a bit.

It was an unusual morning because a cousin had called who also had trauma in her life and we were on the phone for almost an hour. This was the first time she told me so much about her story and how my stepdad had been an integral part of her life as well. This was the first sign because I do not usually stay on the phone when I need to get somewhere, especially somewhere as important as to see dad. It was as if she was delaying me from going. I was anxious to get going so I got in the truck and totally forgot the shovel, bag, etc. Sign number two. I ran inside, ensured that I got everything I needed, and proceeded down our road. Items started falling off the seat and I could hear dad telling me not to come because it wasn't the right time, and it was too dangerous. I was very determined and told him to relax. I had driven in storms many times. As I put my arm out to stop items from falling, I just missed a hydro pole and hit the ditch. I wasn't very far from home, but I did have to call Robin for help to get the truck out. He ended up backing right into said pole, damaging the whole side of the truck. I felt awful but he said patiently, "It's only a truck, be careful." This was sign number three directly from dad almost yelling at me asking, "What do I have to do to make you listen! It's too dangerous and not the time yet. Stay home safe!" I was angry now because what would he know about what I had been through during my life without him? A little too late dad to be trying to parent me! I got back in the truck, got to the end of the road, turned onto the main road, and only went about a hundred feet when I stopped and broke down crying like a little girl. I couldn't stop crying. All the anger, loss, feelings of abandonment, and regrets had disappeared. I realized my dad will always be with me in spirit and this won't change. Every time I look in the mirror, I see him. Every time I see an eagle flying overhead, he is looking out for me. This is the power of tantric healing. He is part of me, heart and soul. I don't remember how long I rested there. Eventually I told him "Thank you for watching out for me all these years," amongst other things. I turned around and went home. I didn't go inside. I went to our special place in the yard where he and my paternal family like to stay.

Every time I see an eagle flying overhead, my dad is looking out for me. What I needed was to deeply start believing in myself. I knew this would take more work than I realized. As I got deeper into healing another layer, I had to revisit old wounds. The hard part is remembering the context of those wounds as you try to put them behind you, and the emotions that went along with them. The amazing part is that I know I have conquered some of them completely because they are not coming up anymore. I have healed some of them at a specific layer I needed to before, so I can do it again, even deeper. This is the power of tantric healing.

There is a special area where only I know what goes on spiritually and the importance of preserving the wild grapes and rose bushes that surround it (my grandmother made amazing wine I was told). There is a special tree for dad, grandmother, and Stephan. Miraculously, when we first bought the property there was a lot of landscaping to do. My son told me specifically as he touched the two trees which represent dad and my grandmother, that we need to keep these two trees. Another tree represents my dear Stephan in the park area that I am creating. My children have inherited my strength and many other gifts that they are not aware of yet. I am proud that we saved these two trees as they are with me daily in meditation.

By this point dad and I had gotten to know each other quite well and could relate to each other easily. He was a welcome guest, and I would often feel him around the house or property. Though, he did know the boundaries of the house that I set for him. As a spirit I told him he was allowed anywhere except the bedrooms as I drew an invisible line at a staircase he was not allowed to cross. This was private for Robin and me. He respected my boundaries because he was glad that he could be in my life in some form, finally. I had gotten the news for the third time that he was not my biological father. I was beside myself and went running to the bathroom to be alone. I was angry because I knew in my heart and soul that he was my dad. This was the first and only time he ran to me beyond my boundary trying to console me. I told him to stay out! Had I gone mad, talking to spirits and soul energy like it was a normal thing? I yelled at him, asking who he really was and what a cruel trick it was to prey on someone's emotions like he had. He left and I never saw him reading the newspaper again. He crossed the line, and he would never do it again.

He respected me more than I respected myself. I called my mom. I was not very respectful of anything she had been through, and I didn't care. I told her that the third test was negative. I could hear her shock on the other end of the line. She swore up and down with maybe one percent chance, then no...one hundred ten percent that Theodore Aguesse is my father. That was when we did the saliva test. I was so completely sure, as I had learned to trust in myself, that Ted was my dad. This turning point for me changed my life forever. When I am feeling weak a deer will present itself to me as if to remind me, "It's okay, you got this." Then I feel stronger, ready to face whatever the universe presents to me again. There are energies and powers at work that I cannot explain and will not even try to. I have enormous gratitude for all my fellow colleagues who have helped along the way via podcasts, coaching sessions, and their friendship. I have crossed paths and walked with some amazing people from all over the world. I would never have come as far as I have without tantric and universal guidance. I am extremely blessed and will continue to thrive beyond even my expectations!

Here are a few wise lessons coaching taught me:

1. Put my oxygen mask on first, otherwise I am no use to anyone else. I am my #1 priority! NO GUILT.
2. Do not take things personally. Everyone is going through something that you may not be aware of. NO JUDGEMENT.
3. Do not assume something about someone. This will cause you to be misinformed and may cause unnecessary drama or gossip.
4. Love does make the world a better place.
5. Every challenge provides a lesson. How you interpret that lesson will provide the next challenge. Stay open by surrendering.

The Other Pauline is a story about a little girl whose courage and determination exceeded her expectations! The primary challenge of not knowing my biological father proved to make my journey an uphill battle that I was not expecting when I chose to accept the role from my ancestors of breaking the generational, traumatic chains that held my families back from success. I thrived beyond every test that was put in front of me to become the successful woman I am today! I candidly share my story of healing to empower others and further break any residual links (or judgements) that people may have. By learning to trust my intuition, aided by my Tantric Shaman Amba Kahly Su, not only was I able to get to know my paternal family, I also learned how to trust in myself. I continue to share my message of self-faith through speaking events and walking with others on their path. Being able to impact people globally so that they feel whole and can live their best life is my purpose on Earth. What is yours?

www.pauline.grouette@guidedjourneycoaching.ca
https://calendly.com/paulinesguidedjourney
www.linkedin.com/in/pauline-grouette-11a8ba216
https://instagram.com/guidedjourneycoaching
https://www.facebook.com/pjgrouette

My gift to you,

a book list that got me through the hardest times and gave me the confidence and direction that I needed…before meeting Amba.

- I always had a **journal** on hand. Interestingly, my mom gave me my first one when I was about eight years old.
- *The Courage to Heal; For Women and Men Survivors of Child Sexual Abuse*- Laura Davis
- *The Courage to Heal Workbook*- Laura Davis
- *What To Expect When You're Expecting*- Heidi Murkoff
- *What To Expect The First Year*- Heidi Murkoff
- *The Gift of ADHD*-Lara Honos-Webb
- *The 7 Habits of Highly Effective People*- Stephen R. Covey
- *You Are Awesome*- Neil Pasricha (I also had the *Awesome Journal*)
- *Leader Without a Title*- Robin Sharma
- *5am Club*- Robin Sharma
- *Think Like A Monk*- Jay Shetty
- *You Are a Badass*- Jen Sincero
- *The Four Agreements*- Don Miguel Ruiz

There were many that I could have included as self-help books to survive, though these provided the most direction FOR ME.

Lesson Learned- you don't need to purchase tons of books with slightly different content. When it comes down to the basics, they have the same message. The difference is the way the message speaks to you and it will be different for everyone. Therefore, if you find two or three that truly speak to you:

1. First read skim to see if it speaks to you.
2. Read deeper to fully grasp the content.
3. Put the message to work for you as you apply it to your journey.

Study it. When you read it multiple times, you will get a different message each time because you will have grown since last reading. Allow yourself to grow and heal. You deserve it!

Learn from my hard lessons so you don't have to struggle.

Sending love and respect to you always,
Pauline

Remainder of the front step on the original Aguesse
homestead in Deerhorn, Mb. 2022

BECOME WHOLE AUTHENTICALLY!
With Guided Journey Coaching and Pauline Grouette

Guided Journey Coaching and Consulting was created
by Pauline Grouette in 2021 when she saw the need to help women
and men become whole on a personal level. She furthered her dream
of creating a comfortable, inviting environment for dental offices
throughout the continental United States and Canada. She facilitates
Vision Board Workshops, 1:1, and group coaching to guide you, or
your team, to make your dreams a reality.

Through telling her story via podcasts, interviews, becoming a
#1 best-selling co-author, and motivational speaker, people
worldwide have overcome limiting beliefs, feelings of loss, conquered
adversity, and developed self-confidence to reconnect with who they
truly are.

Dental offices have brought integrity to the word team as the ripple
effect guides employee's to become their best selves. Guided Journey
Coaching & Consulting walks beside you to empower and celebrate
each milestone.

Guided Journey
Coaching & Consulting

Guided Journey Coaching meets you where you are currently and helps remove the blocks that are in the way for a safe journey. Whether you are looking for personal or professional growth, you set the pace.

For more information about working together, having an office assessment, or vision board workshop for you and/or your team, contact pauline.grouette@guidedjourneycoaching.ca

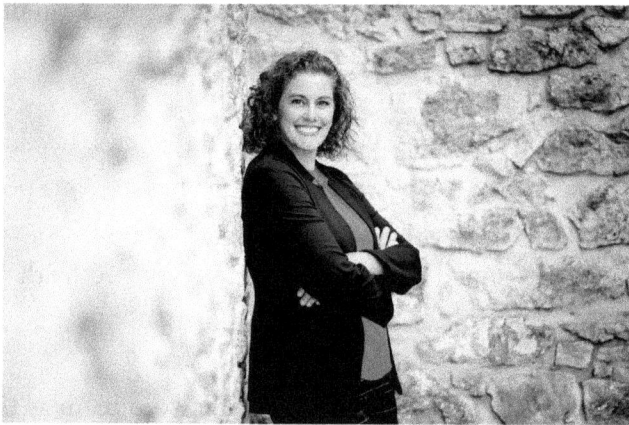

It is never too late to start making your dreams a reality!
www.guidedjourneycoaching.ca

www.ingramcontent.com/pod-product-compliance
Lightning Source LLC
Chambersburg PA
CBHW060238030426
42335CB00014B/1509